I0797154

Embroidery
HANDBOOK
FOR BEGINNERS

Originally published as *La Broderie Pour les Débutants* by Éditions Eyrolles, Paris, ©2019, 2023.

Translated from the French by Ordentop Agency

Library of Congress Control Number: 2024952908

Cover design by Lindsay Hess

Photo credits: DMC (page 8, right-hand column; page 9; page 10; page 12, right-hand column; page 13; page 22; page 23, left-hand column); Les Beaux Arts du Fil (page 11; page 70, left-hand column; page 80); Katrin Wiens (page 12, left-hand column; page 14; page 70, right-hand column); Shutterstock (page 71, Evgeniya369; page 76, Nancy Tripp Photography; page 79, Marina Lesnitskaya).

Type set in: Festivo Letters No.1/Local Brewery/Pluto Condensed/Gauntlet Classic/Archer

ISBN: 978-0-7643-6964-3
ePub: 978-1-5073-0626-0

Printed in India

10 9 8 7 6 5 4 3 2 1

Published by Schiffer Craft
An imprint of Schiffer Publishing, Ltd.
4880 Lower Valley Road
Atglen, PA 19310
Phone: (610) 593-1777; Fax: (610) 593-2002
Email: Info@schifferbooks.com
Web: www.schifferbooks.com

Embroidery HANDBOOK FOR BEGINNERS

AN ILLUSTRATED GUIDE TO TOOLS, TECHNIQUES + STITCHES

CATHERINE GUIDICELLI

CONTENTS

CHAPTER 1: Tools and Materials 7

Basic Equipment 8

Embroidery Hoops 8

Fabric 8
- Embroidery Canvas 8
- Aïda Cloth 9
- Linen Embroidery Canvas 9
- Etamine Embroidery Canvas 10
- Magic Canvas 10
- Other Fabrics 11

Threads 12
- Mouline Embroidery Thread 13
- Perle Cotton 13
- Other Threads 13

Needles 13

Art & Drawing Materials 14

Craft Materials 14

Organization 14
- Threads 14
- Ribbons 15
- Needles 15
- Beads and Sequins 15
- Fabrics 15

CHAPTER 2: Basic Techniques 17

Choosing a Design 18
- Difficulty of Designs 18
- Different Designs 18

Understanding a Design 22
- Design Directions 22
- Grids 22
- Patterns 23

Preparing the Backing 23
- Washing and Ironing the Fabric 23
- Cutting the Fabric 24
- Overcasting the Edges 24
- Putting on Canvas 24

Replicating a Design 25
- Checking Pattern Dimensions 25
- Tracing Directly on Canvas 26
- Tracing the Pattern 26

Placing Fabric in the Hoop 29

Assembling a Mini Hoop 30

Preparing the Thread 31
- Unwinding the Skein Thread 31
- Separating Strands 32
- Threading the Needle 32

Two Ways to Embroider 33
- In One Motion 33
- In Two Motions 33

Raised Work 33

Start and Finish Your Piece Correctly 34
- Blocking the Thread at the Beginning 34
- Ending Stitches 35

Practice Before You Start 35

CHAPTER 3: The 25 Basic Stitches 37

Tracing Edges: Line Stitches 38
- The Running Stitch 38
- The Open Backstitch 38
- The Backstitch 39
- The Chain Stitch 39
- The Stem Stitch 39
- The Double Whipped Running Stitch 40
- Couching 41

Embroidering Small Designs: Individual Stitches 41
- The Straight Stitch 41
- The Sheaf Stitch 42
- The Double Rice Stitch 43
- The Cross Stitch (and Variations) 44
- The Star Stitch 45
- The Web Stitch 46
- The Fern Stitch 47
- The Single Fly Stitch 47
- The Lazy Daisy Stitch 48
- The French Knot 48

To Create Borders 49
The Blanket Stitch 49
The Buttonhole Stitch 49
The Feather Stitch 50
The Persian or Plaited Stitch 52

Filling Stitches 53
The Darning Stitch 53
The Long-Armed Cross Stitch 53
The Half Cross Stitch 54
The Satin Stitch (and Variations) 56
The Lattice Stitch 57

CHAPTER 4: Finishing Touches 59

Washing 60

Shaping 60

Creating Neat Edges 60
Surfacing 60
Hemming Edges 61
Sewing a Bias 61

Ironing 62

Framing 62

Hoop Art 64

Hiding Knots 65

Hiding a Stain 65

CHAPTER 5: Special Embroidery Techniques 67

Ribbon Embroidery 68

Beads and Sequins 68
Embroidering Beads 69
Embroidering Sequins 70

Needlepoint 71
Which Canvas? 71
Which Technique? 71
Which Stitches? 71

The Punch Needle 72
The Different Stitches 72
How to Embroider 73

Appliqué 74

Stumpwork 76
Attached Embroidery 76
Detached Embroidery 76

Quilting 77

Cutwork Embroidery 78

Drawn-Thread Embroidery 79
How to Draw Threads 79
How to Stitch Drawn Threads 79

Smocking 81
Creating the Gathers 81
Embroidering 82

Machine Embroidery 83
The Embroidery Machine 83
The Domestic Sewing Machine 83

Appendixes 85
Stitch-Count Conversion Table 87
Solutions to Common Problems 88
Partnerships and Acknowledgments 89
Index 90

TOOLS AND MATERIALS

When you're just starting out, it's hard to find your way around the wide range of products available at craft stores. Follow this guide to learn to recognize fabrics, threads, and needles and to find out which is the best material for embroidery.

BASIC EQUIPMENT

Embroidery can be done with very few supplies. Here's a list of what you'll need to get started:

- Thick cotton canvas (in white, in color, or even with a pattern)
- Cotton or perle cotton thread
- An embroidery needle with a large eye and pointed tip. For example, the size 24 "chenille" needle is suitable for all embroidery threads.
- A 5.9-inch-diameter hoop
- Small, sharp scissors
- a chalk pencil or, better still, a water-soluble felt-tip marker

STARTER KITS

Kits are very practical if you don't want to invest in all the necessary materials right away. Everything you need to start embroidering is included: the support, threads, and needles. There's a wide range of supports: bibs, sponge towels, case . . . You'll find them in craft stores or online stores, such as DMC.

EMBROIDERY HOOPS

Embroidery hoops (or hoops) consist of two interlocking wooden hoops. Once the fabric has been wedged between the two hoops, a screw is used to tension it sufficiently. Once the embroidery is complete, the canvas is removed from the hoop and reused for a new embroidery, unless you want to follow the hoop art trend (see next box).

Start with a medium-sized hoop (5.9 in.), which will be sufficient for your first embroideries.

HOOP ART

The current trend is to leave the embroidery in the hoop and hang it on the wall like a picture (see page 64). In this case, buy them in sets of several sizes, and you'll pay less.

FABRIC

Embroidery can be done on any type of support, but canvas dedicated to this practice is more suitable, especially for counted stitch, because its weave is very regular.

Embroidery canvas

Embroidery canvases have very regular weaves that allow you to count the threads in the fabric. They are characterized by the number of threads or stitches per inch.

The finer the weave, the more precise and refined the result, but the longer it takes to complete.

THREADS PER INCH AND STITCHES PER INCH DS PER INCH (THREAD/IN.)

- *These measurements indicate the number of threads per centimeter or stitches that can be embroidered in 0.39 in.*
- *For linen or cheesecloth fabrics (unifil fabrics), it's a question of thread per 0.39 in. For example, on a 12-thread linen canvas, there are 12 threads for every 0.39 in.*
- *For Aïda cloth (several threads grouped together), we talk in terms of stitches per 0.39 in. On 5.5-thread Aïda cloth, there are 5.5 stitches for every 0.39 in.*

Please note that English measurements are different. A table at the back of this book will help you convert them. (See page 86.)

Aïda cloth

Ideal for beginners, the Aïda cloth is specially designed for cross stitch and counted stitch. Its threads, grouped in fours, form squares, and the holes are clearly visible: one cross is embroidered per square.

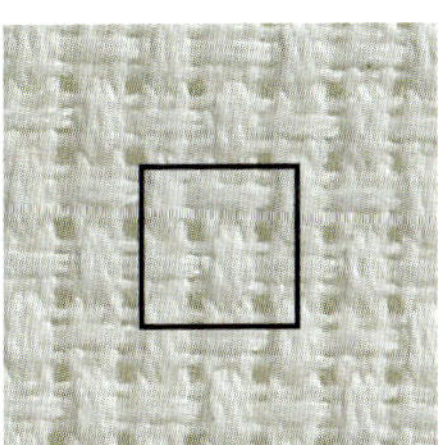

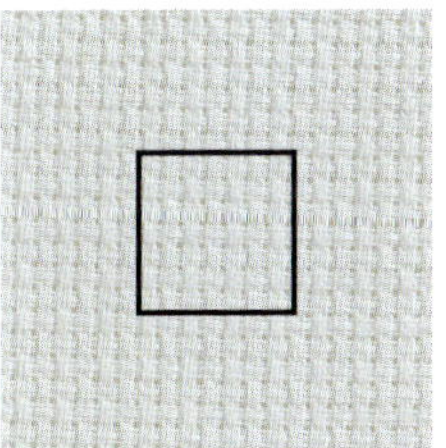

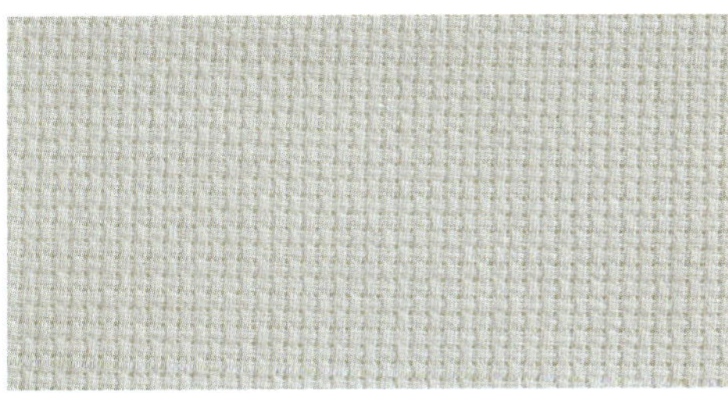

Aïda cloths, 2.4 pts./in. and 7 pts./in.

It's available in different colors and stitch sizes per inch: from 2.4 stitches/in. for the coarsest to 7 stitches/in. for the finest.

Linen embroidery canvas

Linen embroidery canvas is perfect both for free-motion and counted-stitch embroidery. It is available in a wide range of colors, and its natural, matte appearance is very elegant. Unlike Aïda cloth, its threads are not grouped together; it's a unifil fabric. Holes are also harder to find.

It's available in 11 or 12 threads/in.

Linen, 11 threads/in.

Etamine embroidery canvas

This unifil cotton canvas is easier to embroider than linen because its threads are more regular; 10 or 11 threads/in. are available.

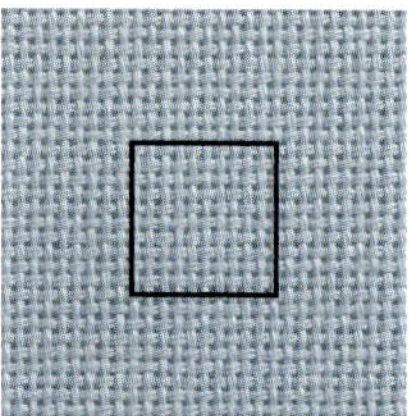

Etamine, 11 threads/in.

Magic canvas

There are also some very clever canvases.

- **Thread-pulling canvas:** For cross stitch embroidery on any surface. Sew it to the garment in large stitches, embroider, and remove the threads from the fabric one by one.
- **Soluble embroidery fabric:** For cross stitch embroidery on any surface. No need to pull the threads one by one—just run it under water! Its only drawback—it's a bit expensive.
- **The Magic Guide:** A grid, which can be washed away with water, is printed on this canvas. Handy for finding your way around!

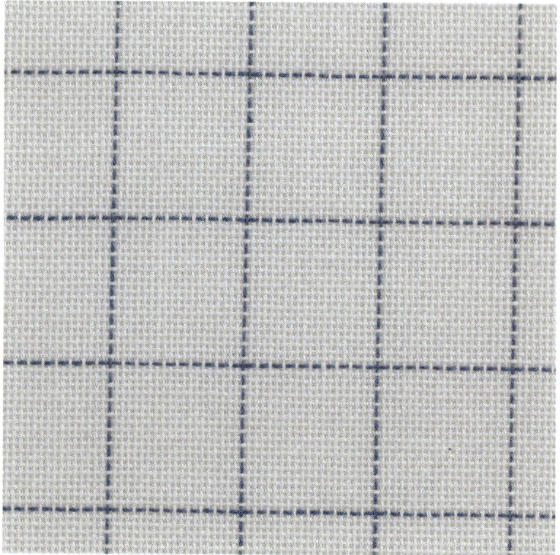

Magic Guide canvas

- **Painted canvas:** Printed with the design, so you don't need to embroider it all over.

Painted canvas from a DMC kit

HOW TO CALCULATE CANVAS SIZE

For counted-stitch embroidery, the grid indicates the number of stitches in height and width, but not the dimensions of the design, which depend on the fabric weave chosen. It is therefore necessary to first determine the size of the fabric required to embroider the design in its entirety. Two pieces of information are required: the design width and the number of stitches per centimeter of fabric.

Start by counting the number of dots on the grid, then divide by the number of dots per round of your canvas. For example, for the Aïda canvas:

- *Pattern width: 50 stitches*
- *Number of stitches per inch: 5.4*
- *Pattern width in inch: 50 ÷ 5.4 = 9.25*

Make the same calculation for the height. Don't forget to leave a margin around the design if you wish to frame it.

If the fabric is linen, do the same calculation with the number of threads per inch, but halve the figure if you're embroidering on two threads.

Fortunately, for those who are not good with numbers, there are online calculators!

https://yarntree.com/java/xstitchcal.htm

https://www.thread-bare.com/tools/cross-stitch-fabric-size-calculator

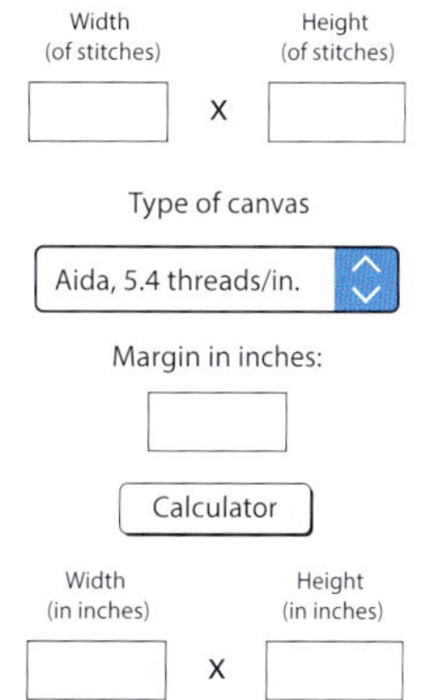

Other fabrics

You can embroider on all types of fabric: cotton, jute, denim . . . but beware: unlike special embroidery fabrics, their threads are tight and therefore difficult to distinguish. So it's best to use them for free-motion embroidery.

- **Cotton:** The thicker it is, the easier it is to embroider. What's more, it won't warp. For printed cottons, help yourself to patterns.
- **Transparent fabrics:** For light, airy embroidery. Be careful to hide the threads on the back for a neat result.
- **Tarlatan:** This starched gauze is thick and rigid. It is ideal for embroidery because it does not deform.
- **Tulle:** With white thread, the embroidery imitates dentil. In this case, work with very fine threads.

Luneville embroidery with pearls created by Les Beaux Arts du Fil

- **Stretchy (or loose) fabrics:** These should be reinforced beforehand with an iron-on fabric (see page 24) to facilitate embroidery. If you wish to retain the fabric's suppleness, you can remove it after embroidery.

CANVAS FABRIC

Rigid and with large holes, canvas is ideal for tapestries and rugs made from wool, not embroidery! It is, however, suitable for children, as its weft is very thick.

The possibilities are endless! Leather, paper, cork, etc.—anything goes! And with a little experience, you'll be able to embroider on clothes, bags, napkins, cushions . . . Give free rein to your creativity.

Embroidery on leather with silk organza applique (design by Katrin Wiens)

TIP

To get started, choose a solid fabric with a dense weft (at least 11 threads/in.), especially if your embroidery includes heavy elements such as beads or ribbons.

THREADS

Thread is made up of several strands. Depending on the size of the thread used (i.e., the number of strands chosen), the final appearance of the embroidery will vary. The smaller the design, the finer the thread.

But don't embroider with just any thread! Go for embroidery threads that won't wear out or fade.

The paper rings around the thread skeins indicate the thread brand, quality (e.g., Mouline Special), thread size, color reference (e.g., 4190), and washing instructions.

COLOR MATCHING

Threads come in an infinite number of colors. Brands define each of their colors by a specific reference, and embroidery patterns indicate which threads to buy in a certain brand. If your fabric store doesn't sell the recommended color, you'll have trouble finding the same color in another brand. To help you, color-correspondence charts between brands are available on the internet.

Mouline embroidery thread

This is the most common thread. Silky and shiny in appearance, mouline embroidery thread is sold in a single size, made up of six strands that can be separated easily. Depending on the desired embroidery effect, you can work with one, two, or three strands.

Be careful—the strands can separate and get in the way while you're embroidering. Don't make the needles too large.

Perle cotton

Twisted, perle cotton is ideal for beginners, since its strands do not separate. It adds relief to the embroidery: the stitches are clearly visible.

It is sold in sizes 3 to 12. It's best to start with number 5 thread, which is quite thick.

Other threads

Here are just a few examples of other threads.

- **Special embroidery thread:** Very easy to work with, and its four strands don't tangle. It is slightly finer than mouline and perle cotton.
- **Twisted wool and cotton:** Thicker, ideal for canvas and tapestry
- **Glossy yarns:** There are sequined, metallic, silk, and even gold yarns. Slippery, they are difficult to embroider. They should be washed at low temperatures, since they are more fragile.
- **Machine embroidery thread, 100% mercerized cotton:** This is the thread for machine embroidery.

WHAT IS MERCERIZED COTTON YARN?

Invented in the 19th century, this is a chemical treatment designed to make cotton smoother, more receptive to dyeing, and glossier.

NEEDLES

Embroidery needles are wide and have a large eye, adapted to the thickness of the thread to be embroidered. They pull the threads away from the fabric, allowing the thread to pass through without wearing.

Needle numbers indicate the size of the needle. The higher the number, the finer the needle. Your choice of needle depends on the fabric and thread you're using.

- **Embroidery needles** (pointed tip)
  - sizes 1 to 10
  - for all fabrics
  - for ground threads from six strands (needle no. 1) to one strand (needle no. 10)
- **Tapestry needles** (pointed tip)
  - sizes 18 to 26
  - for all threads and fabrics they can pierce easily
- **Cross-stitch needles** (round tip)
  - sizes 22 to 26
  - mainly for Aïda cloth, to be inserted between threads

- **Fine pearl needles:** Suitable for all fabrics. The only constraint is that the eye and thread must pass through the hole in the bead.
- **The magic needle** (or punch needle, see page 72): This is a tubular needle through which the thread passes, making it easy to embroider loops.

> **NOTE**
>
> **Start with the larger needles. You can also buy two sets of different needles, round-tipped and pointed. Experiment with thread and fabric, and you'll always find the right one!**

ART & DRAWING MATERIALS

For transferring patterns, tracing paper and special fabric carbon paper are useful. Magic Paper (see page 28) is a self-adhesive paper that dissolves in water, making it easy to use.

To trace the pattern on the canvas, a simple black or white chalk pencil, depending on whether your fabric is light or dark, will do the trick. Water-soluble markers are also available.

You'll also need a ruler to take measurements, and tape and pins to secure the designs to be transferred.

CRAFT MATERIALS

- **Two pairs of scissors:** small, sharp ones for cutting thread and making days, and large ones for cutting fabric
- **Fabric glue** to fix the embroidery permanently to the hoop and to reinforce the knots at the back
- **Iron-on fabric or stabilizer** to stiffen the fabric or hide the back of the embroidery
- **A thimble** to avoid pricking your fingers, and a needle threader
- Beads, sequins, buttons, ribbons for ribbon embroidery, fabric scraps for appliqués: anything is possible to personalize your work!

ORGANIZATION

Sequin embroidery samples (by Katrin Wiens)

To save time (and money too!), I recommend tidying up your equipment.

Threads

Arrange your skeins of yarn in a shoebox, neatly lined up and sorted by color.

If you have a large number of skeins, sort them into transparent freezer bags by color harmony, or into binder pockets (make a yarn binder!).

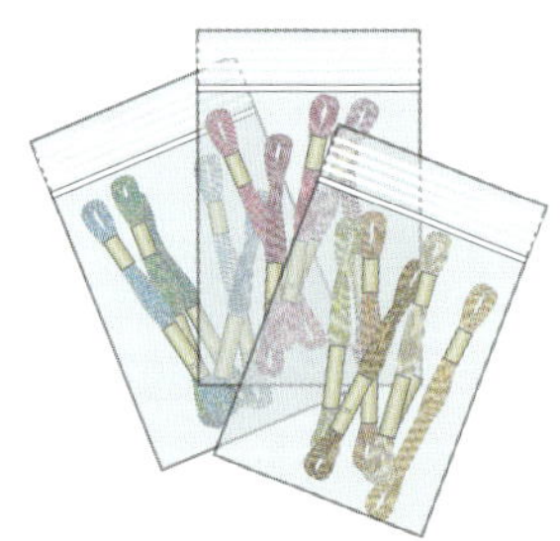

While you're working, put any thread scraps away in a jam jar to avoid scattering them everywhere or getting them stuck to your clothes

Fabrics

Hang fabrics on hangers. They will stay tidy and will be easier to find.

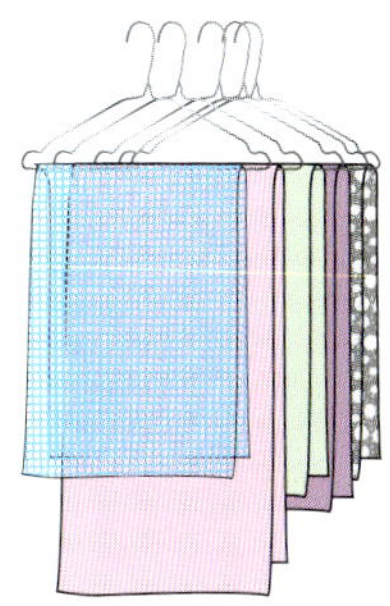

TIP

Keep the labels on opened skeins: You won't need to look up the brand and reference number of the thread if you need to buy more.

Ribbons

Wrap ribbons around cardboard strips and store them in boxes or clear plastic bags.

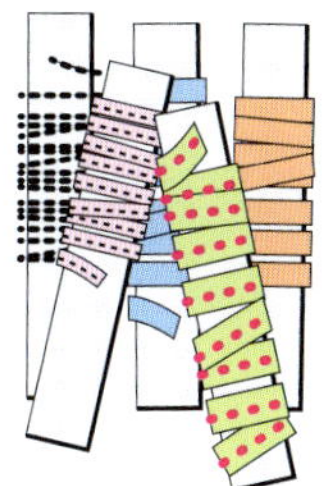

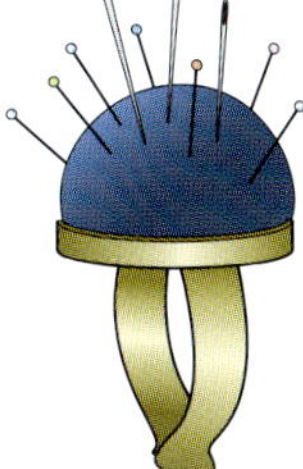

Needles

Stick the needles and pins onto a small cushion you've made or onto a needle bracelet sold in the trade. There are some very handy magnetic ones.

Beads and sequins

Keep the transparent food trays to store larger materials (buttons, large beads, etc.). Buy storage boxes in DIY stores.

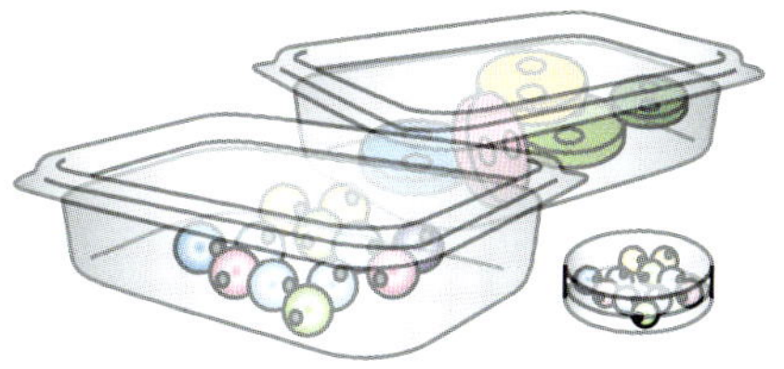

WHEN IT'S TIME TO EMBROIDER

The best thing is to prepare your materials in advance, so you don't have to stop because you're missing a thread color or needle size.

- *At home, place all your embroidery materials on a tray. Leave it there until the work is finished.*
- *Away from home, it's best to pack your supplies in a dedicated bag. That way, you'll always have it on hand. Use transparent kits of different sizes for threads, scissors and pencils, bead boxes, and needle picks.*

I advise you not to leave the embroidery in the hoop. Wrap it inside out, in fabric, around a cardboard tube. Carry it on the tube in a fabric bag. Above all, don't fold it, since this will mark the creases.

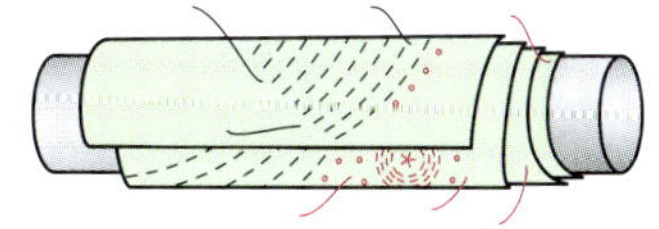

BASIC TECHNIQUES

When it comes to embroidery, a few basics are necessary to avoid mistakes and save time. Familiarize yourself with the techniques you need to know: choosing and transferring a design, creating your own design, preparing threads, etc.

CHOOSING A DESIGN

When you think embroidery, you think design. The first step is to select the right design. To do this, ask yourself what you're going to use your design for. Do you want to decorate a garment or a cushion or simply create a picture to adorn one of your walls?

KNOW YOUR TERMS

Don't confuse the terms design, model, and pattern.

- *The design is the artwork you are going to embroider.*
- *The model contains all the explanations.*
- *The pattern is a "plan" of the embroidery.*

Different designs

There are many different types of designs: cross-stitch, text, alphabet, monograms or simple illustrations. Thread manufacturers have many to offer, but you can also create your own.

Creating your own design

If you can't find what you're looking for among the many designs available in catalogs or on the internet, why not embroider your own design? It's great fun and a great idea for personalized gifts.

1. Outline a photo, a child's drawing, a handwritten text.
2. Reduce or enlarge the design so that it fits perfectly into the shape on which you want to embroider it.
3. Transfer the design to the fabric, using the technique of your choice (see page 25).

Difficulty of designs

The difficulty of embroidery depends on several factors.

- The backing (fabric). Special fabrics sold for embroidery are easier to work with: They are rigid and their weft is clearly visible (see page 8). To make sure you don't damage a garment you want to embroider, try out a similar fabric first.
- The size of the design. This is more a question of speed of execution than difficulty. If you're a beginner and work slowly, pre-fabricate a small format (3.9 x 3.9 in. maximum) or a border, which will embroider more quickly.
- The stitches. Choose a design using a limited number of basic stitches: you'll have less to learn!

Note that the patterns indicate, as an aid, the level of difficulty and the completion time.

To start with, I advise you to embroider on a hoop or on an easy-to-find and inexpensive backing, such as a tote bag. That way, you won't risk damaging an item of clothing that's important to you if your embroidery isn't successful! Choose a simple design with large shapes, few surfaces to fill, and a limited number of stitches.

You can also use stencils or cookie cutters to easily draw simple designs such as stars or flowers.

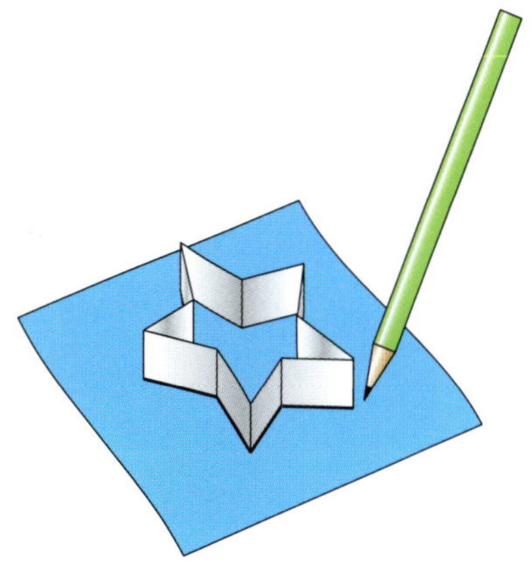

CREATE YOUR OWN CROSS STITCH PATTERN

To make a cross stitch pattern yourself, turn it into colored squares.

1. *Draw a grid with squares the same size as those on your canvas.*
2. *Draw the design in the grid.*
3. *Color the squares with the thread colors you want to use.*
4. *Embroider the fabric, following the grid.*

To help you, the Pic2pat.com website converts your photos or drawings into cross stitch grids. Enter the embroidery format, the number of stitches per inch, and the thread mark. The site then generates a grid and tells you the number of colors needed.

Painting on canvas

You don't have to embroider the whole design you have imagined. To add color, simply paint (before or after embroidering) certain parts of the canvas. Before you start, try out a sample of the chosen canvas to test the colors and texture of the paint.

- If the backing is intended to be washed, use fabric paint and iron it on according to the manufacturer's instructions.
- If the embroidery will be purely decorative, simple gouache or even felt-tip pens will do the trick.

> **TIP**
>
> **If you don't like the result, hide the paint by embroidering with a stitch that covers it (see page 56.)**

Embroidering texts

Text is an essential part of embroidery, whether you're embroidering an alphabet sampler, embroidering a phrase on a garment, or personalizing a gift with a first name.

The alphabet sampler

Often made in cross stitch, this is a classic. It represents an alphabet, each letter more or less ornate. It is usually given as a baby shower gift or as a picture to hang in the baby's bedroom.

Simple text

Simply trace the letter at the stitching point (see page 39).

Use large stitches for straight lines and smaller stitches for rounded areas. For thicker text, embroider it in stem stitch (see page 39).

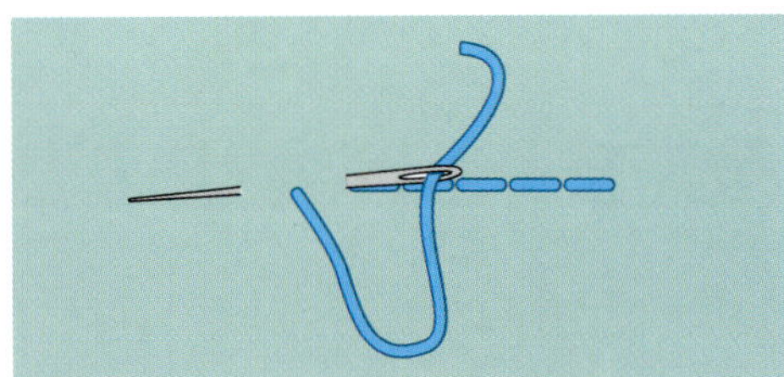

Backstitch

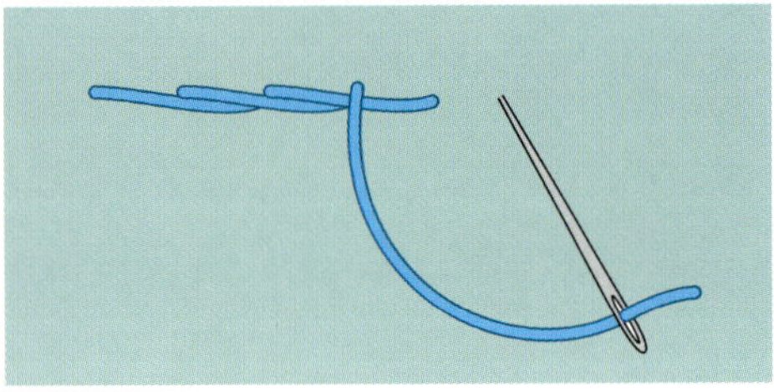

Stem stitch

The monogram

A monogram is an emblem made up of interlaced initials. Passed down from generation to generation, it was often embroidered on household and table linen.

Embroider the outlines in backstitch (see page 38), then fill in the inside of the wide parts in flatlock stitch (see page 56).

Using your own text

When embroidering text, the typeface you choose is obviously important. You can use your own handwriting or use one from software such as Word. If the standard software doesn't have the font you want, download it from a specialist site (e.g., dafont.com, fontsquirrel.com, whatfontis.com). Then simply install it on your computer.

> **TIP**
>
> **Choose fonts that are copyright-free, so you don't have to pay for them.**

What typeface should you choose? It depends on the size of the word to be embroidered. Opt for simple, linear typefaces for texts less than ¾ inch high. For a monogram over ¾ inch, more elaborate typefaces with solid and unconsolidated strokes are ideal.

There are typefaces in which the letters are replaced by symbols: stars, hearts, etc. Use them as designs and not as text.

ABCDEF

Arial Regular corps 36

Times Regular corps 100

- Here are a few examples of free typefaces to download and adapt to your needs.

ABCDEFGHIJKLMNOPQRSTUVWXYZ

Just Another Hand Regular

ABCDEFGHIJKLMNOPQRSTUVWXYZ

Luiss Sans

ABCDEFGHIJKLMNOPQRSTUVWXYZ

BOLICA

ABCDEFGHIJKLMNOPQRSTUVWXYZ

JuanMikes

ABCDEFGHIJKLMNOPQRSTUVWXYZ

Cardenio Modern

ABCDEFGHIJKLMNOPQRSTUVWXYZ

monofur

ABCDEFGHIJKLMNOPQRSTUVWXYZ

Ralphie Brown Regular

abcdefghijklmnopqrstuvwxyz

Strawberry Whipped Cream

- What type size? In typography, the size corresponds to the size of the letter. It can vary depending on the font. For example, in size 36, a letter written in Times measures 10.8 mm compared with 9.1 mm in Courier. Here are some examples of sizes for capital letters in Times and Courier:
  - size 36:. 0.4 in,
  - size 72: 0.8 in.

corps 36

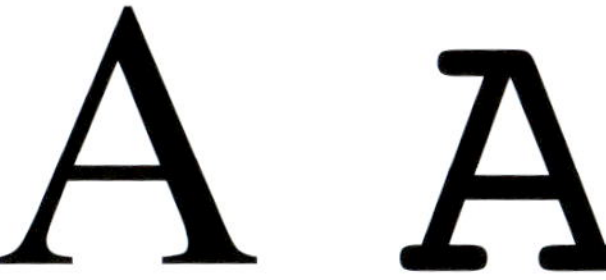

corps 72

MY ADVICE

Since it's difficult to know exactly the final format of the text, enter it directly into your word-processing software and transfer it directly onto your computer screen.

ALPHABET SAMPLER EXAMPLE

The letters in an alphabet sampler must be arranged harmoniously in a chosen format.

1. *Choose a font from your word-processing software or download one.*
2. *Enter the text in your word-processing software. Divide the letters into several lines and center the text.*
3. *Enlarge the letters to the desired size and view your page at 100%.*

ABCDEFG
HIJKLMNO
PQRSTUV
WXYZ

ABCDE
FGHIJK
LMNOP
QRSTU
VWXYZ

4. *Print the text and transfer it to the embroidery fabric, using a pencil or erasable marker.*

UNDERSTANDING A DESIGN

To follow a design, you need to understand the explanations and be able to read a grid. This is essential before you start—if, of course, you haven't decided to create your own design.

Design directions

The directions specify which material (fabric, thread color references) and stitches to use, as well as the finishings to apply after embroidery.

Grids

The counted stitch patterns (cross stitch and petit point) are presented in the form of a grid. Each stitch is indicated by a colored square or a symbol (cross, triangle, square, dot, line, etc.). A legend accompanies the grid, and a grid pattern helps count the stitches.

A horizontal and a vertical line sometimes represent the center of the pattern. If this is the case, locate it with a pen if it is covered by embroidery, or by running a basting thread (which you will remove later) if it remains visible. Start embroidering from this center.

On the grids at the right, the arrow indicates the center.

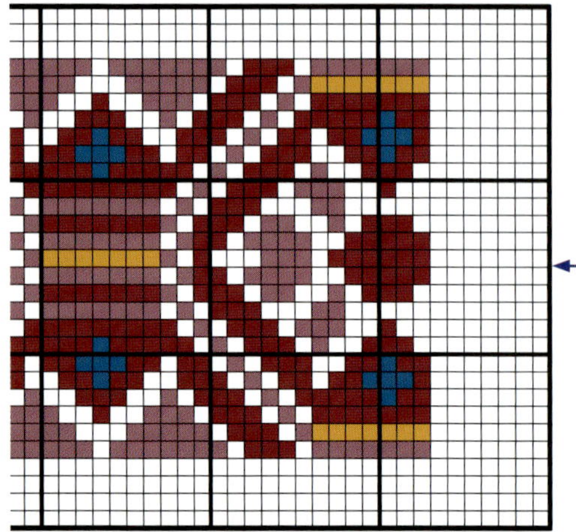

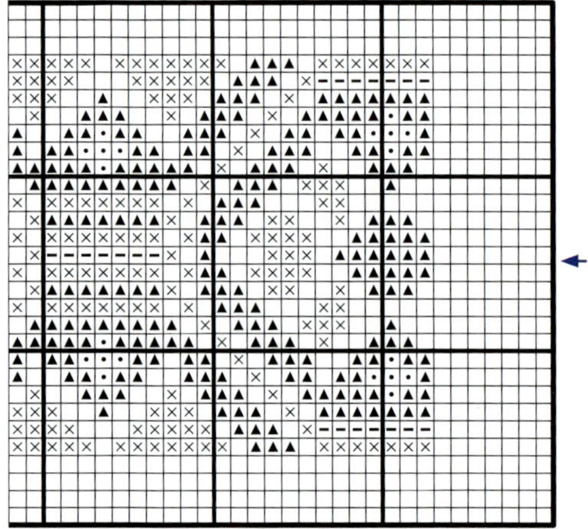

Intermediate cross stitch grids

Patterns

Patterns are created in color or black and white, and they represent the design to be embroidered. Numbers or legends indicate the stitches and thread colors. You will need to transfer them directly if they are to scale 1 (i.e., actual size). If they are not, you will need to reduce or enlarge them (see page 25).

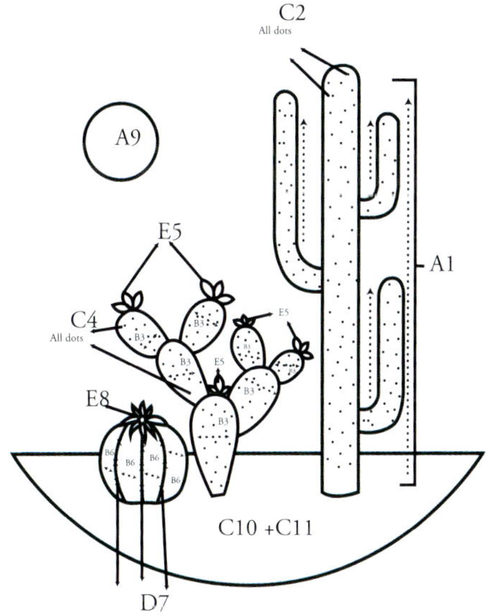

Easy level patterns (DMC)

PREPARING THE BACKING

The backing must be perfectly primed to avoid unpleasant surprises later (i.e., fabric that shrinks, frays, or warps).

Washing and ironing the fabric

Before cutting the fabric, you have two options.

If you want to embroider on a fabric that will be washed afterward (a cushion cover, a tablecloth, a garment, etc.), wash it first to make sure it doesn't bleed or shrink. This is the fastest method for large fabrics, but don't forget the drying time!

For smaller pieces, you can age the fabric: This simulates a wash so that the fabric doesn't move in the future.

1. Iron thoroughly with steam, in the direction of the warp and weft. Don't forget to set the temperature of your iron as indicated on the fabric label.
2. Then iron without steam to dry.

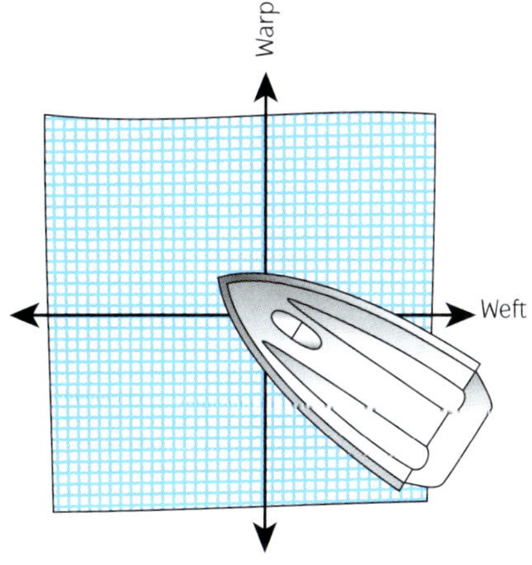

THE WARP AND THE WEFT

Fabric is a weave. The threads stretched vertically on the loom are the warp threads. The horizontal threads that cross them are the weft threads. Iron them so that they remain perpendicular, to avoid distorting the fabric. Threads running in the direction of the warp are called straight threads.

Cutting the fabric

When working in a hoop, cut the fabric to leave a margin of at least 2 inches around the hoop.

For embroidery that will be framed, leave the same margin around the design.

Overcasting the edges

If your fabric frays, overcast the edges before embroidering in hand overlock stitch or machine zigzag stitch.

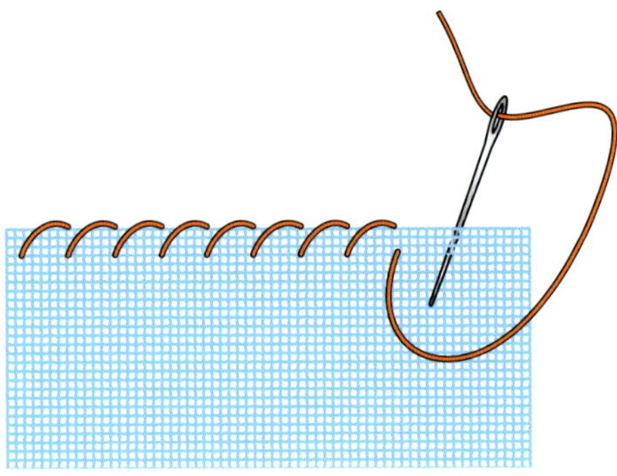

Hand overlock stitch

Putting on canvas

This technique stiffens loose or supple fabrics so that they don't distort when embroidered.

1. Equip yourself with an iron-on canvas. They come in different thicknesses and colors.

IRON-ON INTERFACING

There are woven and nonwoven iron-on interlinings. Woven iron-on is softer and must be cut in the straight line; nonwoven iron-on can be cut in any direction and is ideal for embroidery. Choose the thickness and color that most closely match that of your backing.

2. Place the canvas on the reverse side of the fabric to be embroidered, iron-on side (shiny side) against the fabric.
3. Place a piece of greaseproof paper on top and iron for several seconds, without steam.

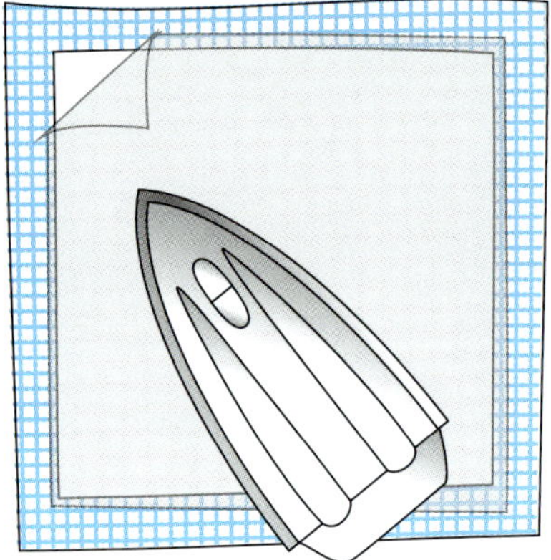

REPLICATING A DESIGN

Before the fabric is inserted into the hoop, the design must be traced. If you're doing counted-stitch embroidery, skip this step, since you'll be counting the stitches by using the grid.

Checking pattern dimensions

To work on a predefined backing, make sure the design is the right size before tracing it. To do this, measure the fabric onto which it will be transferred. Don't forget to leave a margin of a few inches all around the fabric, so that you can place it in the hoop (see page 29). If there isn't enough room, you'll need to make the pattern smaller. Caution: If the pattern is too small, certain details may become illegible and impossible to embroider.

> **NOTE**
>
> **For embroidery on a hoop, the maximum dimensions of the design are those of the inside of the outer ring of the hoop.**

If the pattern is not to scale, enlarge or reduce it, then transfer it to white paper to make a pattern, as explained in the following diagrams.

With a grid

1. Draw a grid every inch on the pattern.

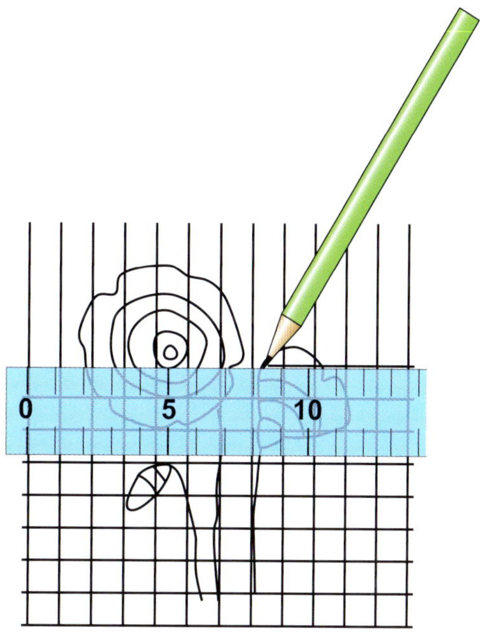

2. Draw a grid to scale on a sheet of paper: If you need to enlarge the pattern twice, enlarge the squares twice..

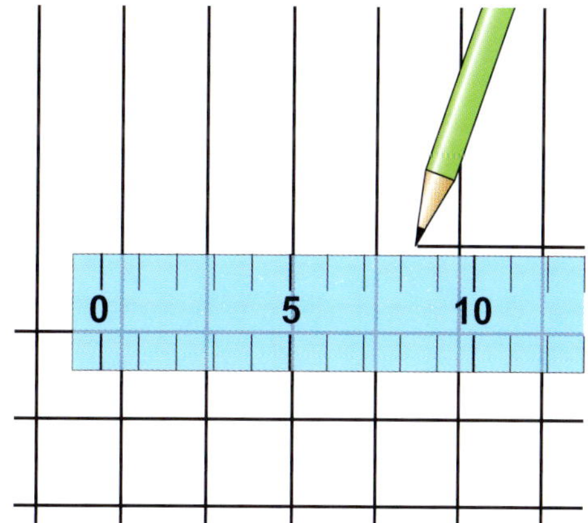

3. Draw the pattern square by square on the new grid.

With a photocopier

Photocopy the design, scaling the size up or down as needed.

CALCULATE THE NECESSARY PERCENTAGE FOR ENLARGEMENT OR REDUCTION

It's a simple rule of 3. Here's an example.

1. *Measure a dimension. For example, the width of pattern A is 3.1 in.*
2. *Define the new width (e.g., B = 4.7 in.). The enlargement percentage is x. The calculation is as follows:*

$x = B \div A \times 100 = \div 8 \times 100 = 150\%$ *enlargement rate.*

For a reduction, the calculation is the same. If A = 4.7 in and B = 3.9 in, x = 66.6% reduction.

X is the number you need to mark on your photocopier.

Tracing directly on canvas

Why not draw your own design (text or a simple design) freehand directly onto the canvas, following your inspiration? With an erasable marker, you'll never have to worry about making a mistake again!

Tracing the pattern

Transparency

If the canvas is light enough or thin enough to see the pattern through, place it on top. Tape it to the table and transfer. If not, attach it to a window.

Be careful with the direction of the thread: Place the design in the direction of the straight thread so as not to distort it afterward.

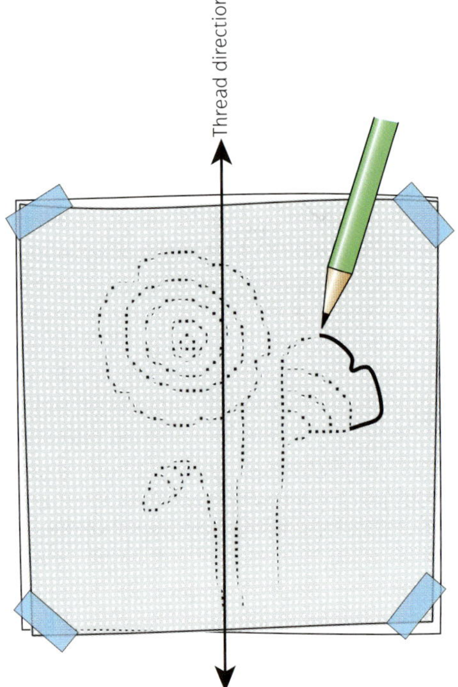

With tracing paper

1. Using tracing paper, offset the pattern with a pencil.
2. Do the same on the reverse side of the tracing paper, using a wax pencil.
3. Place the tracing paper right side up on the canvas, and trace over the design with the pencil, pressing firmly on the outlines.

With carbon paper

This paper is suitable for smooth fabrics such as cotton or tightly woven fabrics (no fewer than 7 threads per 0.39 inch). Choose the color according to the fabric: it must be light enough to see the line clearly.

1. Place the carbon paper between the pattern and the canvas, inked side down.
2. Iron over the pattern, pressing down firmly with a pencil.

You can use a sewing-pattern roller to press on the carbon; its spikes transfer the pattern very easily.

With Magic Paper

Also known as "water-soluble" or "stabilizing" paper, Magic Paper is a self-adhesive (or nonstick) paper that dissolves in water. This technique comes in very handy on dark fabrics, on which pencil or carbon are difficult to see.

1. Trace the design on the paper.
2. Glue or pin to canvas and embroider.
3. Remove the paper by running the fabric under water.

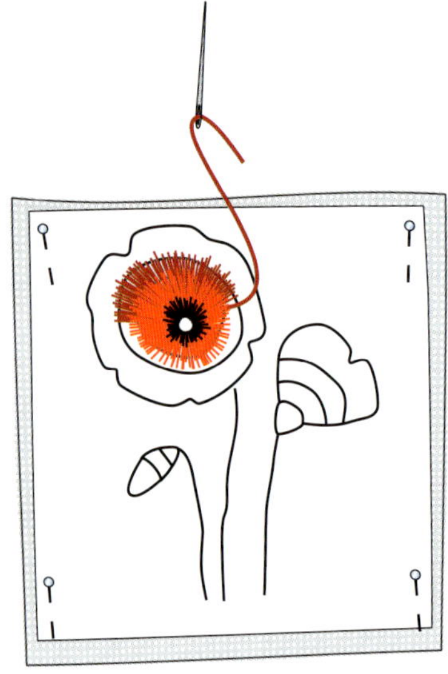

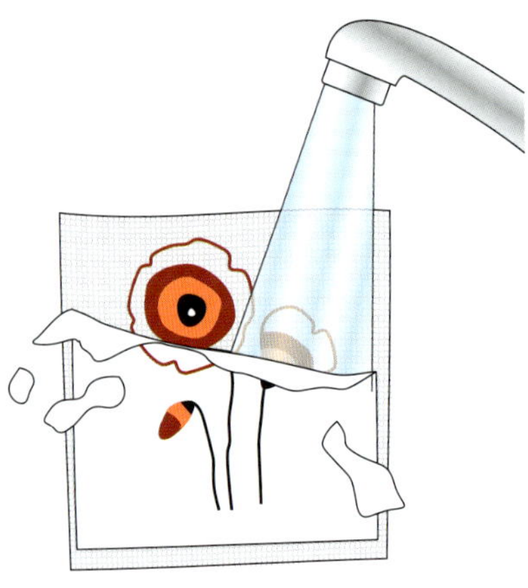

There are designs already printed on Magic Paper. In this case, all you must do is stick them onto the surface of your choice: jeans pocket, shirt collar, napkin, etc.

Quilting

This technique is used to transfer a pattern onto fabric. It is perfect for tight fabrics such as cottons, which mark the holes well, but is not suitable for canvas or embroidery linen.

1. Secure the pattern to the fabric with pins or tape.
2. Using a large needle (or a tracing wheel), stitch on the layout at strategic points (corners, crossings) or following the pattern every 0.39 or 0.78 inch. The holes are transferred to the canvas and serve as reference points.

3. Draw freehand or with a ruler.

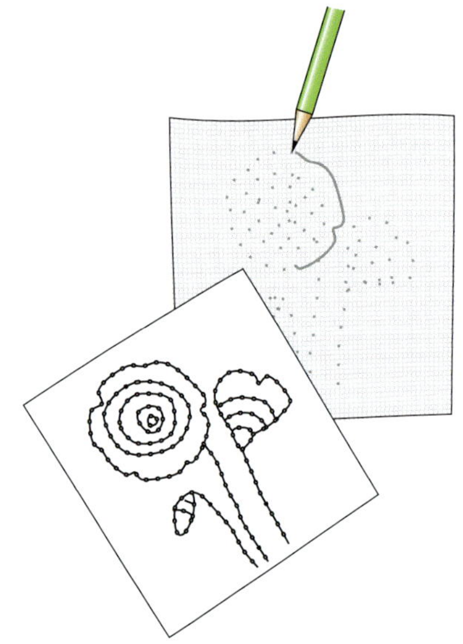

PLACING FABRIC IN THE HOOP

The hoop is almost always a must, since it allows the fabric to be stretched. However, it is not necessary if you're embroidering in one motion (see page 33).

1. Cut a square of fabric, leaving at least 0.78 inch all round the inner ring of the hoop. If you've drawn a design, center it well.

2. Place the fabric on the small ring of the hoop. Loosen the screw and press the outer ring onto the small ring to trap the fabric.

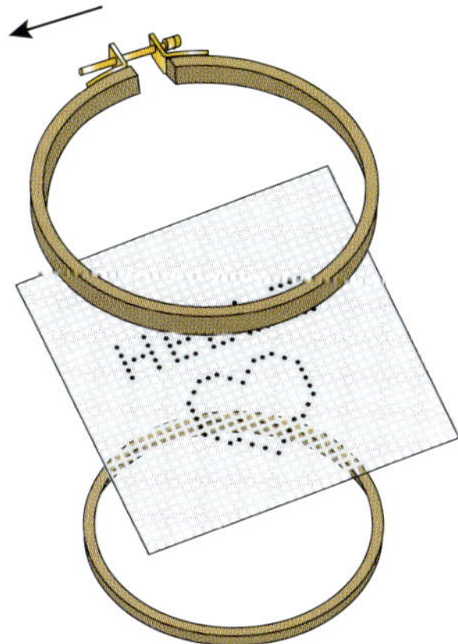

3. Tighten the screw. Pull a little on the fabric to tighten it, but gently, so as not to deform it.

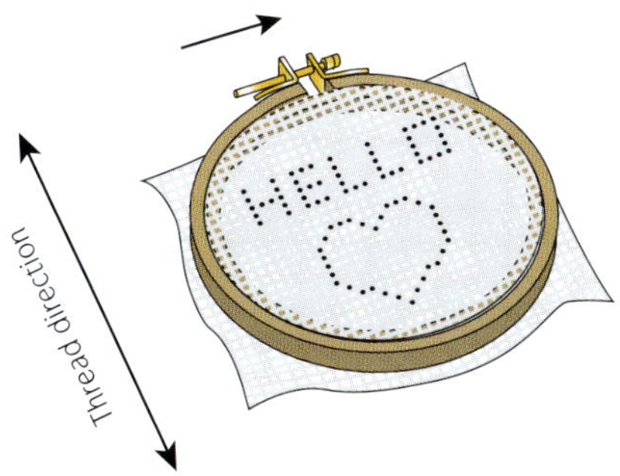

4. Start embroidering. If your design is larger than the hoop, move the fabric as you work.

5. Once the embroidery is complete, remove the large ring and unscrew it to avoid distorting the fabric.

EMBROIDERY ON A GARMENT

If you're working with a hoop, insert the part of the garment to be embroidered. Otherwise, slide a sheet of paper inside the garment to avoid embroidering both layers.

ASSEMBLING A MINI HOOP

Mini hoops consist of a frame, a cardboard support on which to place the fabric to be embroidered, and a cardboard backing to hide the back of the work. A screw and two nuts are used to tighten the frame.

> **NOTE**
>
> **The pattern is not embroidered directly on the mini hoop but on a larger classic hoop (approx. 3.9 inches).**

1. Embroider the pattern on the hoop.

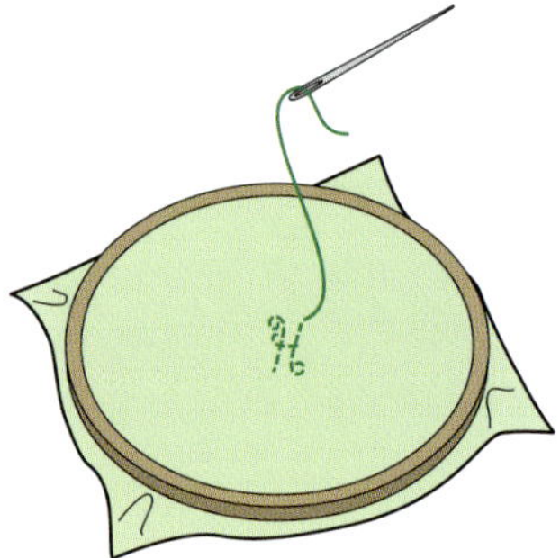

2. Place the mini-hoop frame on the fabric, centering the design, and trace its outline, leaving a 0.78-inch margin.

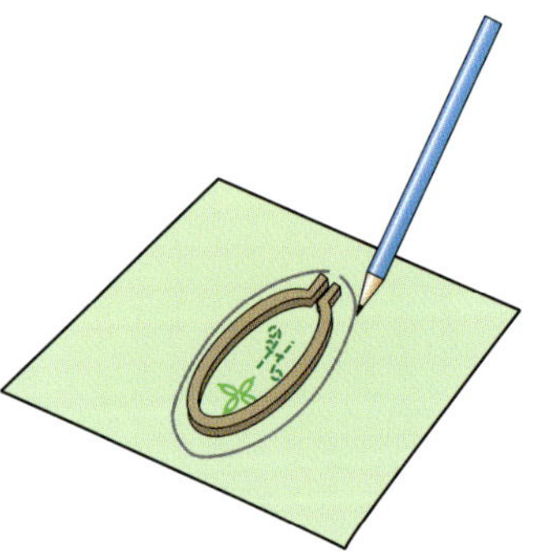

3. Cut the fabric, following the line.

4. Place the fabric on the cardboard of the mini hoop, centering it well.

5. Push the frame over.

6. Tighten the hoop with the screw. Fold the protruding fabric over the reverse side of the cardboard and glue it in place.
7. Glue a cardboard backing over the folded fabric.

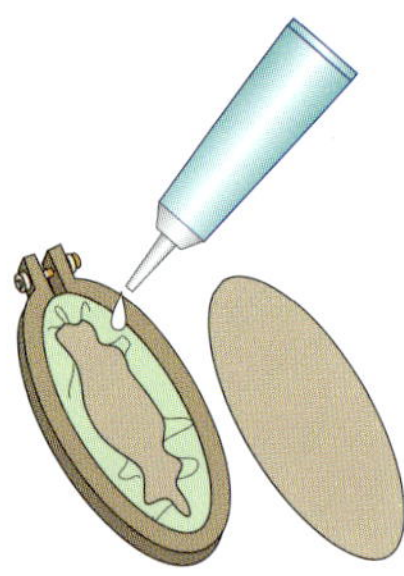

8. Place the first nut on the screw and insert it into the two frames.

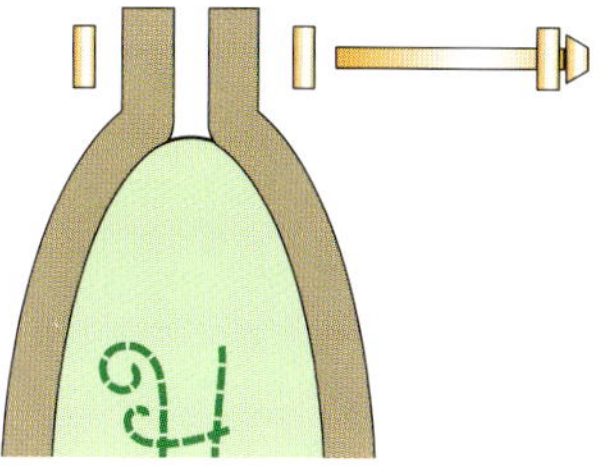

9. Screw on the other nut on the other side to tighten, using your fingers or small pliers.

> **NOTE**
>
> **Do not overtighten the screw, since the wood is brittle and may break.**

10. If the fabric is too thick and the screw too short, remove the first nut.

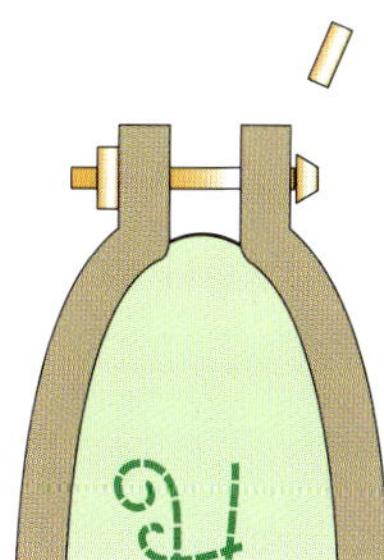

11. To mount the mini hoop, insert a chain on the screw between the two wooden frames. For a brooch, glue the fastener to the back.

PREPARING THE THREAD

Thread comes in skeins surrounded by and held with paper rings.

> **TIP**
>
> **Keep the paper rings around your thread scraps, so you can easily find the color references if you need to touch up your embroidery.**

Unwinding the skein thread

Use skeins no longer than 17.7 inches. Any longer and the thread will tangle and wear during embroidery.

Mouline

Gently pull on the end of the thread so that it unwinds without removing the paper rings.

An unwound length of embroidery thread measures 5.9 inches. Unwind it three times to obtain sufficient length for embroidery.

Perle cotton

Perle cotton is wound around itself and knotted. The resulting ring is then twisted.

Remove the surrounding paper and unfurl the twist. Cut the thread at the knot and unwind to the required length.

HOW TO SAVE YOUR THREAD

Some patterns specify the length of thread to be used. Be careful not to make the thread lengths too short, since starting and stopping consumes thread, but they shouldn't be too long either: Don't go beyond 17.7 inches, to avoid twisting.

Once you've cut a good length of thread and separated it into several strands, keep the remaining strands and roll them up on a small rectangle of paper, so you'll know that each one is the length of a needle.

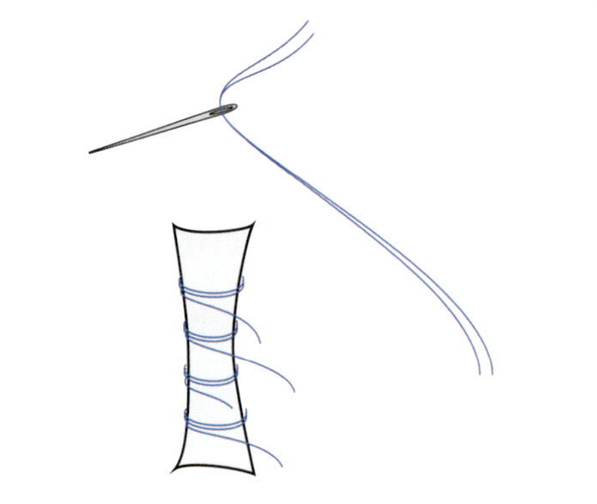

Separating strands

If you don't use all the strands of your thread, grab the necessary number and pull the others down.

Threading the needle

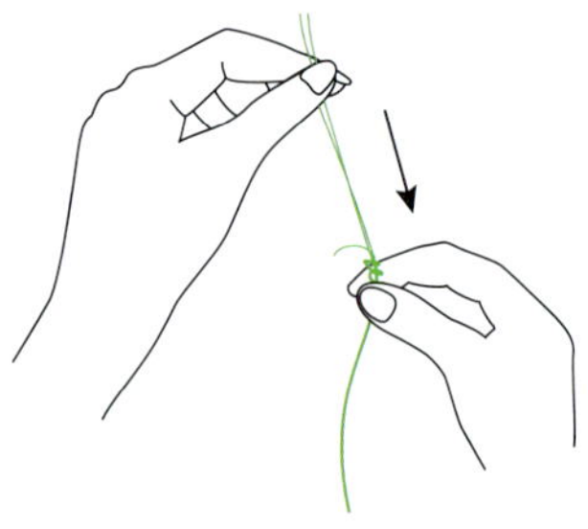

Cut the thread cleanly with scissors. Moisten the end to harden it and hold it between your index finger and thumb. Advance the needle toward the end of the thread.

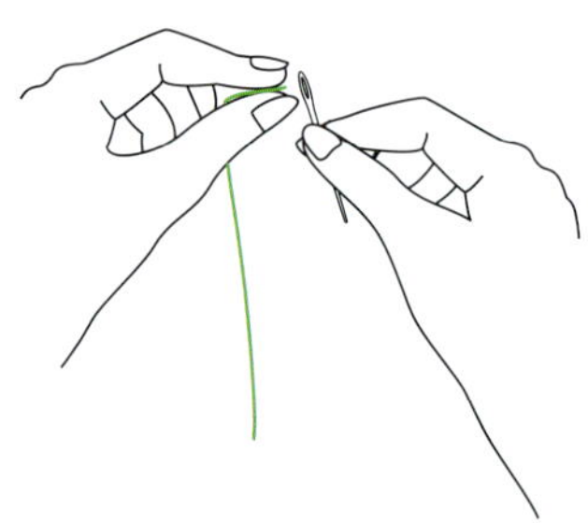

NOTE

To thread the needle more easily, fold the end of the moistened thread in half, twist it, and slide it into the barrel.

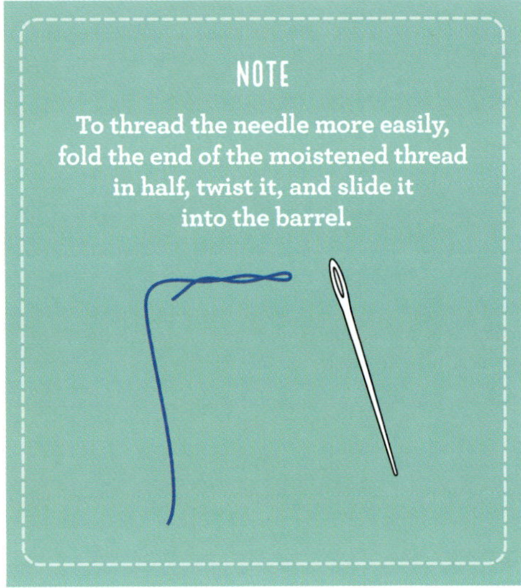

To make the task easier, there are handy needle threaders available: Thread the metal loop through the eye and slide the thread through. Pull on the metal loop, and it pulls the thread through the eye.

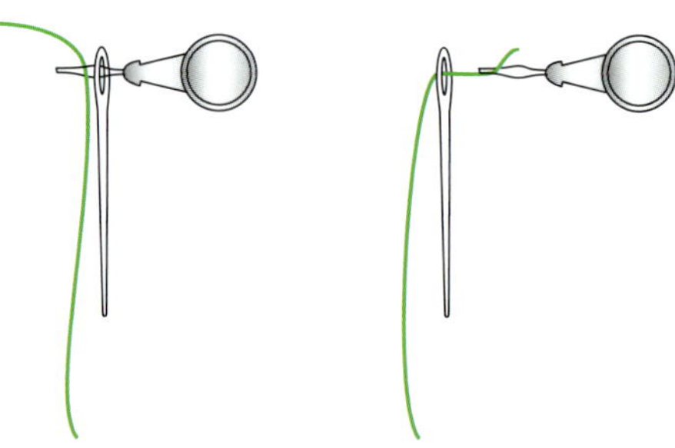

If you don't want to invest in a needle threader, make your own by folding a thin piece of wire or a strip of paper in half.

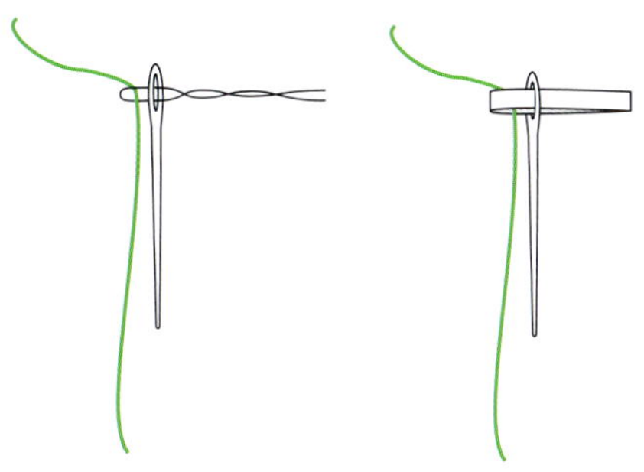

TWO WAYS TO EMBROIDER

There are two ways to embroider: in one motion or in two motions.

In one motion

Simply push the needle in and pull it out in the same motion. To do this, the fabric must not be taut, since you need to pleat it a little.

While this method is faster than the two-motion method, it is also less accurate.

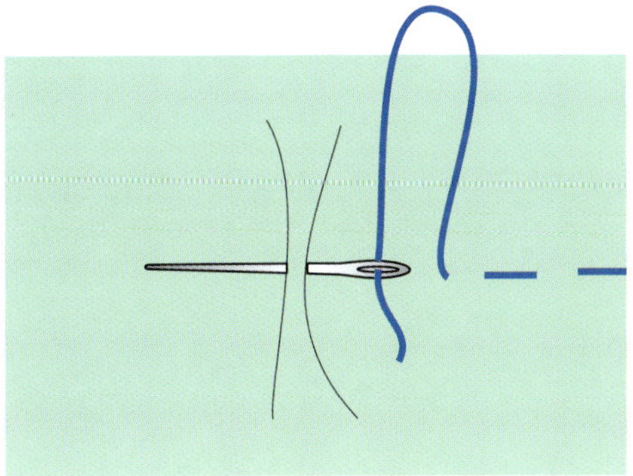

In two motions

This method is mandatory when the fabric is stretched over an embroidery hoop.

1. Stitch the needle vertically and pull it out from the other side of the fabric. Pull on the thread.
2. Stitch the needle and pull it out again on the other side.

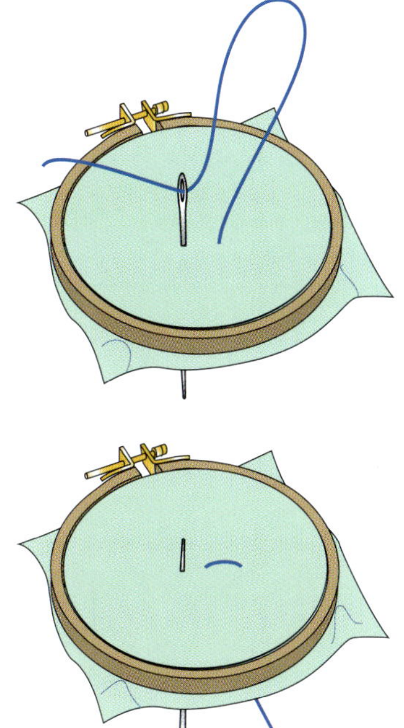

RAISED WORK

Light casts a different light on threads, depending on their direction. Play with the direction of the stitches to create depths.

For cross stitch, always embroider the two cross stitches in the same order, so that the top half stitches are always inclined in the same way.

START AND FINISH YOUR PIECE CORRECTLY

For a clean, solid finish, it's important to stop the threads correctly.

Blocking the thread at the beginning

With a knot

1. Pinch the end of the thread between your thumb and forefinger and roll it over your forefinger.

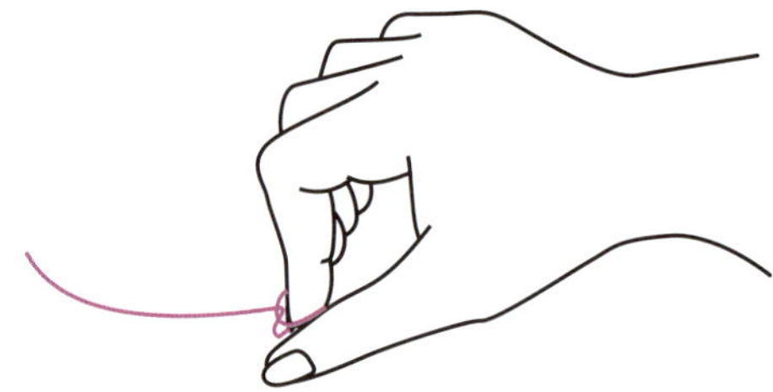

2. Insert the needle on the back of the fabric at the point of the first stitch. Don't pull too hard on the thread, to prevent the knot from cutting through the fabric.
3. Cut the thread, leaving a 0.19-inch overhang.

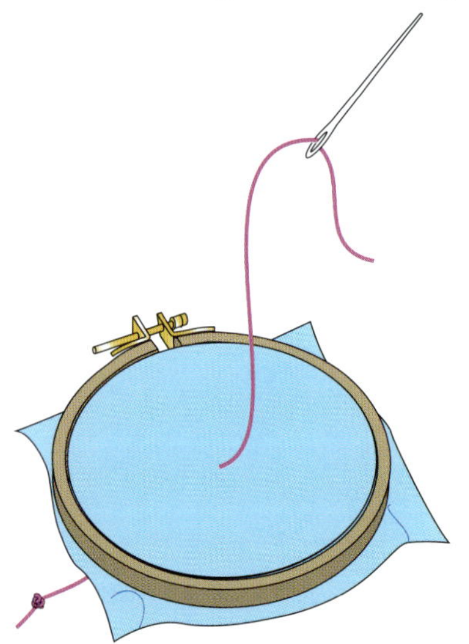

Without a knot

If you need a clean back (e.g., for a napkin), you don't need a knot.

1. Insert the needle on the wrong side 0.78 inch after the start of the pattern, leaving 0.78 inch of thread in reserve.
2. Hold the end of the thread with your finger or a piece of adhesive paper and embroider a few very small front stitches on the right side and larger ones on the wrong side.

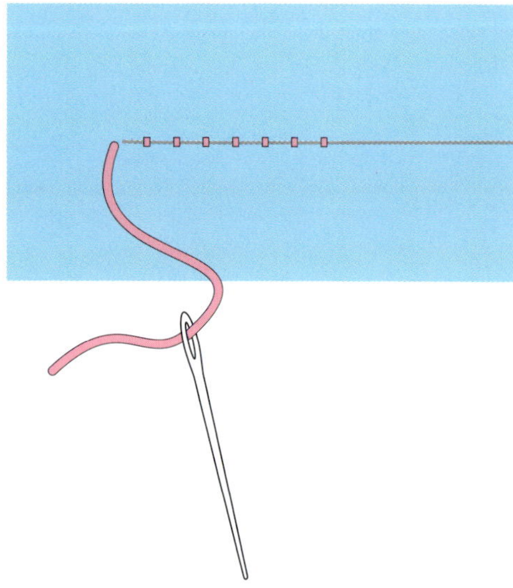

3. Embroider the first stitches over the thread.
4. Cut off the 0.78 inch left on the back of the stitch.

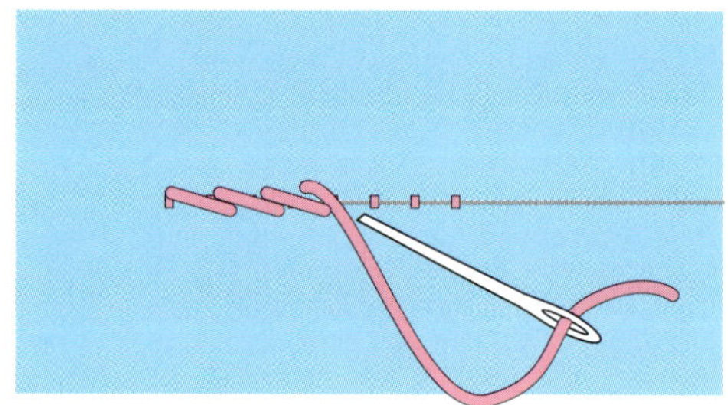

Ending stitches

With a knot

At the end of the embroidery, on the reverse side, slip the thread around the last stitches for 0.78 inch and knot: Form a loop around the end of the thread, pass the needle under the stitch and through the loop at the same time, pulling the thread with your fingers.

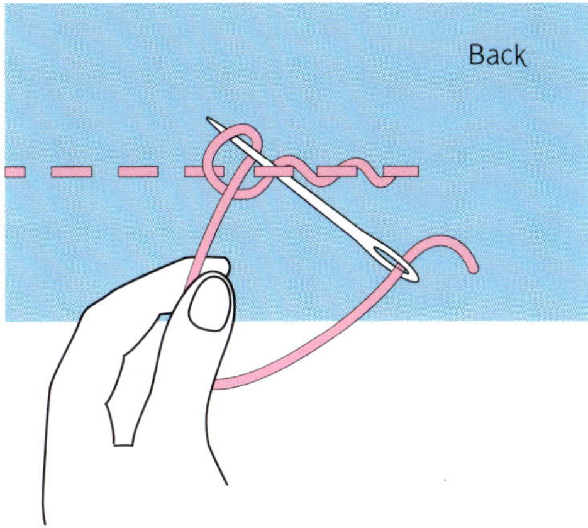

Please note that it is not advisable to make knots on the reverse side of the embroidery if the work is to be washed and ironed. There is a risk that they will unravel and add depth that will mark the fabric when ironed.

Without a knot

Slide the thread around the last stitches as before, then slide it back around the stitches in the opposite direction.

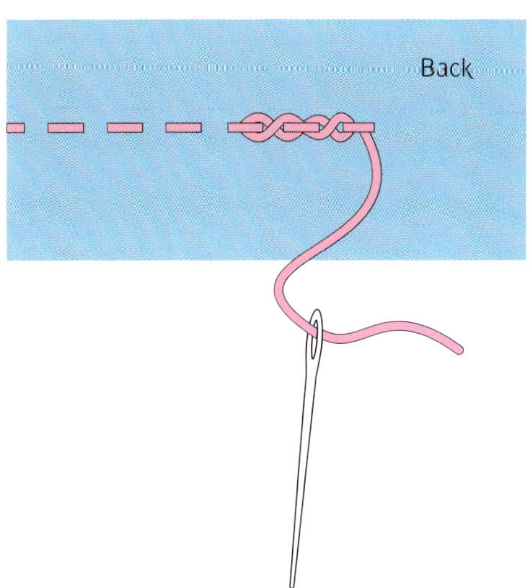

TIP

To be on the safe side, apply a dot of fabric glue to the cut threads.

PRACTICE BEFORE YOU START

Now that you have the basics to start embroidering, you'll be able to learn the most common stitches. But first, practice on scraps of fabric to embroider regular, smaller, and smaller stitches. That's how you'll make beautiful embroidery!!

I recommend starting with large stitches. That way, your work will be more regular.

To check the length of your stitches, make two marks on your thumb.

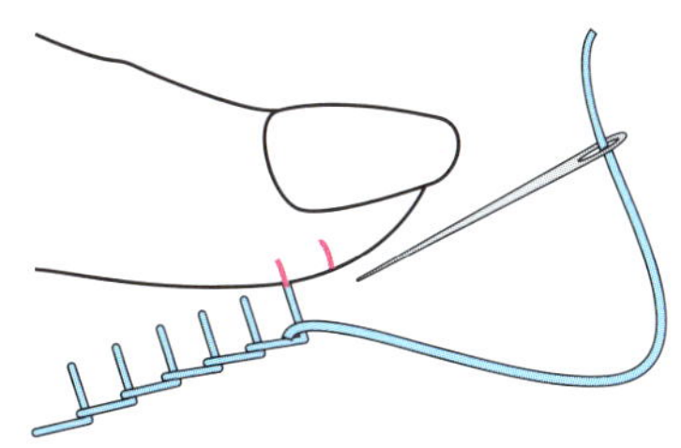

THE 25 BASIC STITCHES

Think of embroidery as a painting with the needle and thread as drawing tools. Some stitches are used for outlining, others for "coloring," and still others for creating small designs. Here are the simplest basic stitches to get you started, sorted by style. Embroider them alone or combine them!

RIGHT SIDE UP OR UPSIDE DOWN

In this book, the drawings show the right side of the fabric, with the knot hidden on the wrong side.

To help you understand the stitches, the needle is shown in its entirety in the explanatory drawings, as if the stitch were made in a single movement. In reality, however, the stitch is made in two movements.

TRACING EDGES: LINE STITCHES

These stitches are used to follow a line (to draw an outline or write a word). They are the simplest stitches.

The running stitch

The running stitch is embroidered from right to left for a dotted effect.

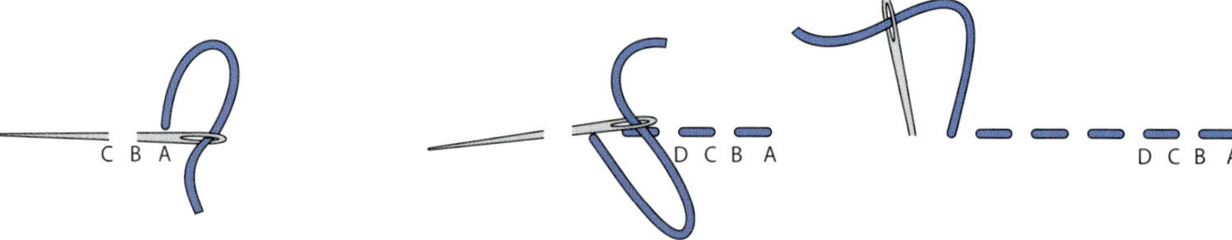

1. Pull the needle out at A. Stitch at B and pull out at C.

2. Stitch in at D and continue using stitches of the same size. The spaces between each stitch can be equal or different lengths.

3. Finish with a running stitch.

The open backstitch

The open backstitch is stronger than the running stitch. It is embroidered from right to left

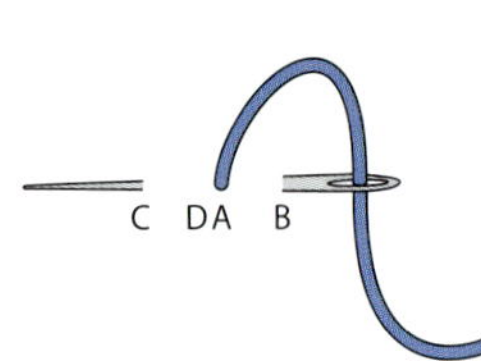

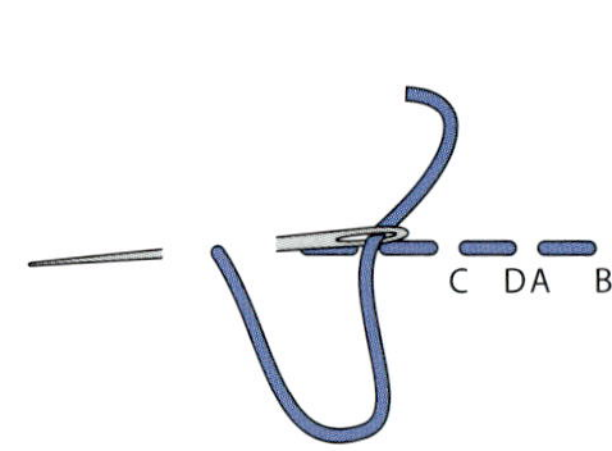

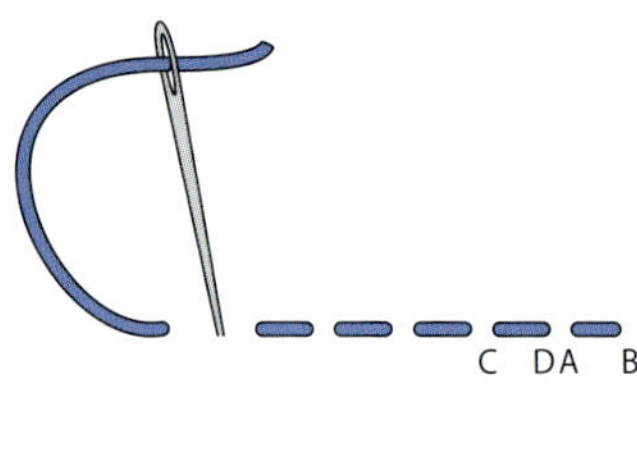

1. Pull the needle out at A. Stitch at B, backward, and pull out at C, forward.

2. Stitch in at D backward and restart. The spaces between each stitch can be equal or different lengths.

3. Finish with an open backstitch.

The backstitch

The backstitch is embroidered in the same way as the backstitch, but without spaces.

1. Follow Step 1 for the open backstitch.

2. Finish, not by stitching at D, but in the hole of the previous stitch.

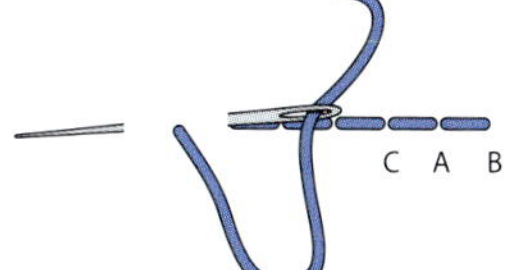

The chain stitch

Thicker than the previous stitches, the chain stitch, with its interlocking loops, is decorative. It can be embroidered from right to left or from top to bottom.

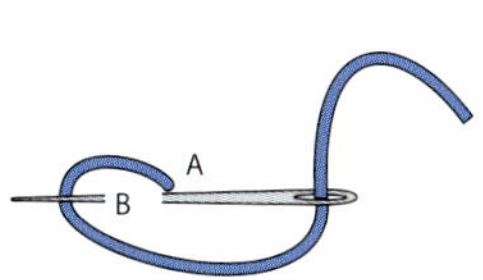

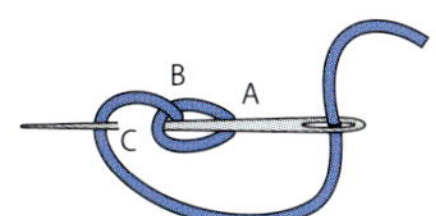

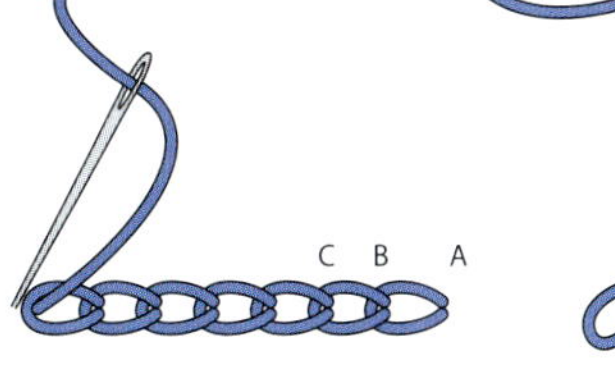

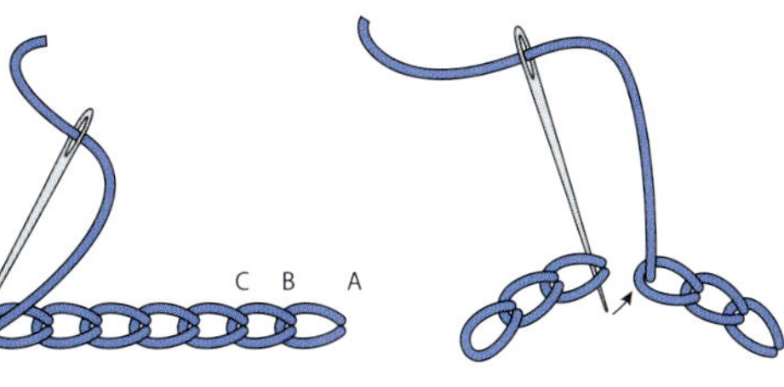

1. Pull the needle out at A. Stitch in the same place and pull out at B, passing the thread under the needle tip to form a loop. Do not pull too hard on the thread.

2. Stitch at B and repeat step 1.

3. Finish by inserting the needle on the other side of the thread to hold the loop in place.

4. If you're embroidering a closed shape, make the last loop under the first loop.

The stem stitch

The stem stitch is embroidered from left to right: The needle advances one stitch and exits in the middle of the stitch above the thread.

Stitches are generally of the same length, except when embroidering a roundel, in which they are shorter.

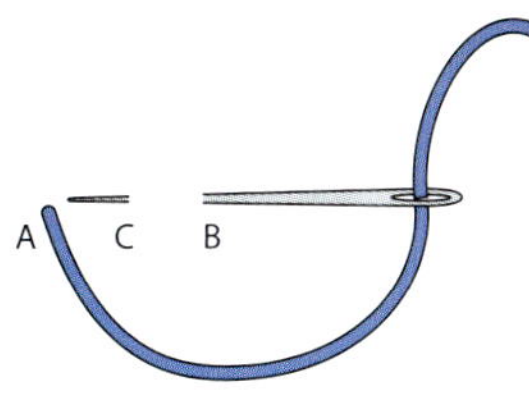

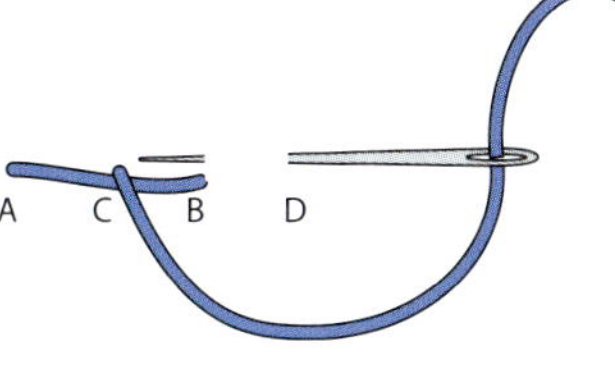

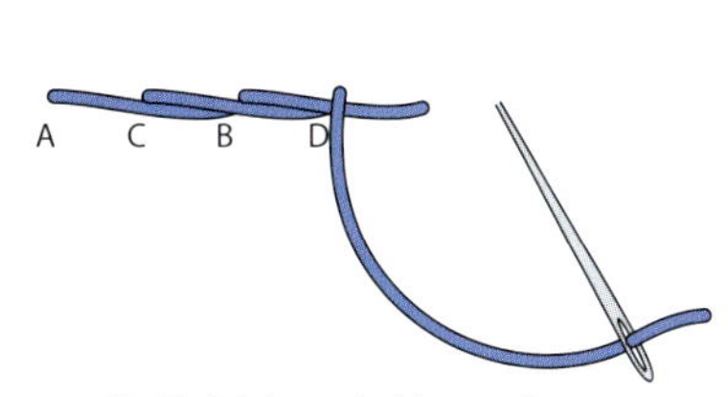

1. Pull the needle out at A. Stitch at B and exit at C (the middle of AB).

2. Stitch at A and exit at B (middle of CD).

3. Finish by stitching at D.

The looped stem stitch

The looped stem stitch is embroidered without stretching the thread between A and B, to form loops. It can be used to create raised work designs.

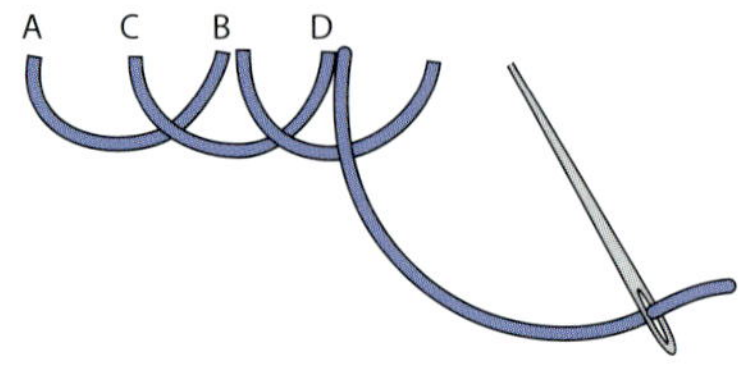

The slip stitch

Unlike with the stem stitch, the needle exits through the thread, not over it.

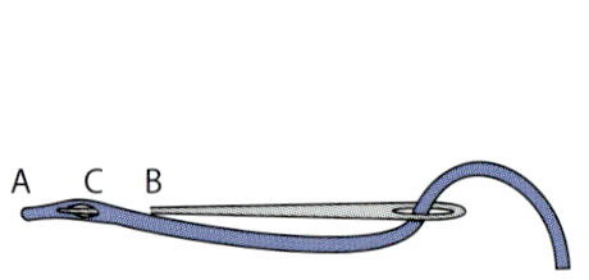

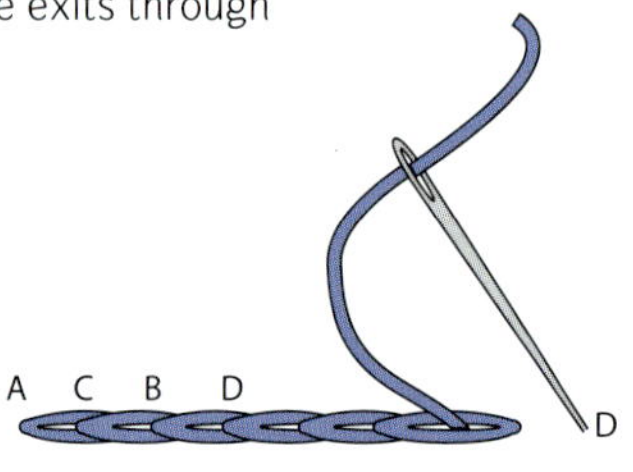

1. Pull the needle out at A. Stitch in at B and exit at C (the middle of AB), then into the thread, which should be taut.
2. Finish by stitching at D.

The double whipped running stitch

This is a running stitch in which you embroider a second thread. With a different-colored thread, it's very decorative. Embroider from right to left.

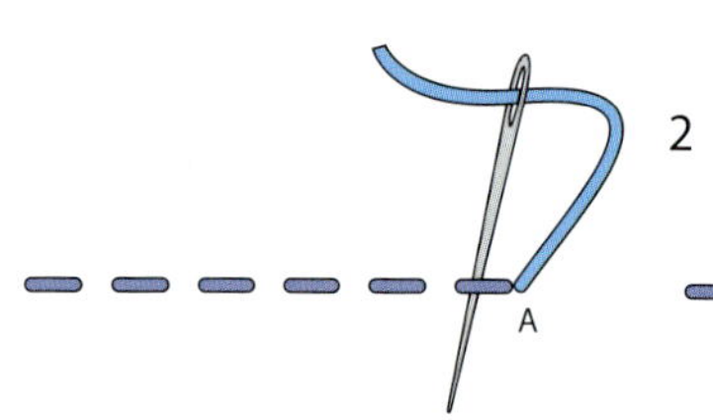

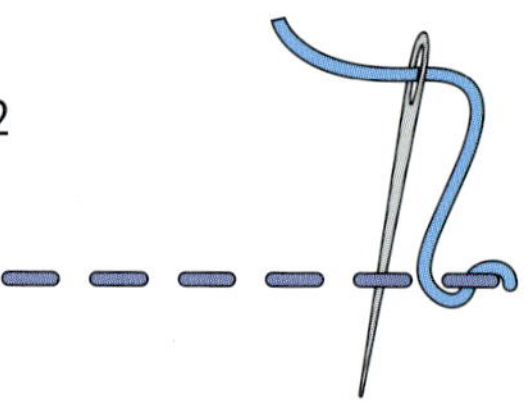

1. Make a running stitch. Take out the needle with the new thread at the end of the first stitch and slide the needle under the thread, from top to bottom. Be careful not to insert the needle into the fabric.
2. Pull up and slide the needle under the next stitch, always working from top to bottom.
3. Finish at the end of the last stitch.

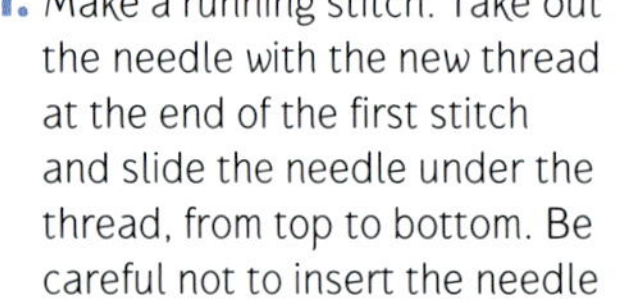

Couching

Couching is embroidered from right to left with two threads.

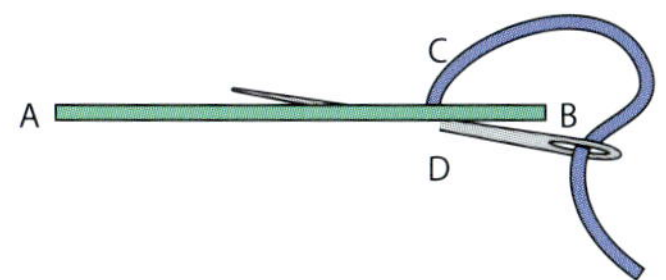

1. With the first thread, make a large stitch from A to B. Bring out the second thread above at C. Stitch underneath vertically at D and pull out farther above at E.

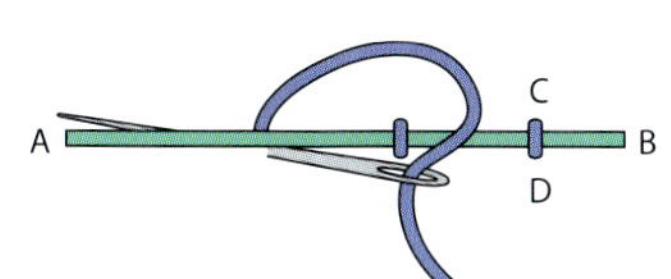

2. Continue with evenly spaced vertical dots.

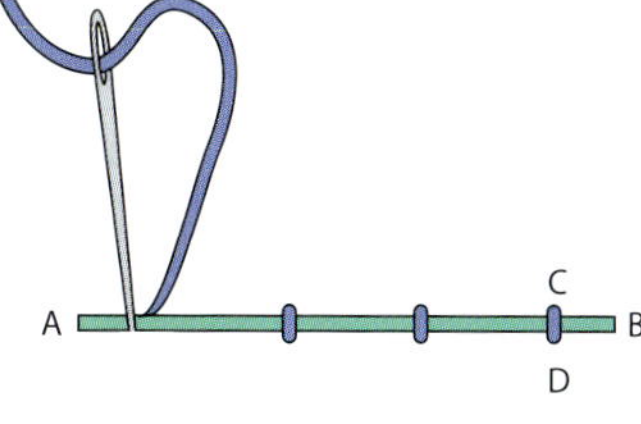

3. Finish by stitching underneath.

EMBROIDERING SMALL DESIGNS: INDIVIDUAL STITCHES

You can embroider these stitches alone as small designs or in groups to fill an outline.

The straight stitch

A very simple stitch, the straight stitch can be embroidered from left to right or right to left. Draw larger or smaller straight lines.

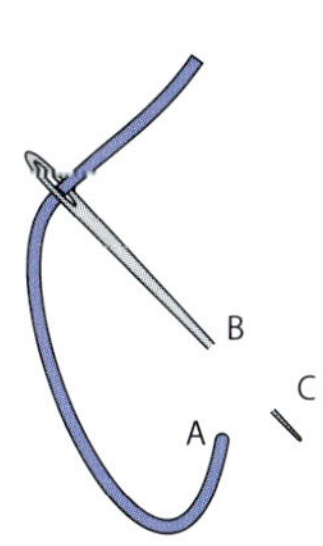

1. Pull the needle out at A. Stitch at B and pull out at C.

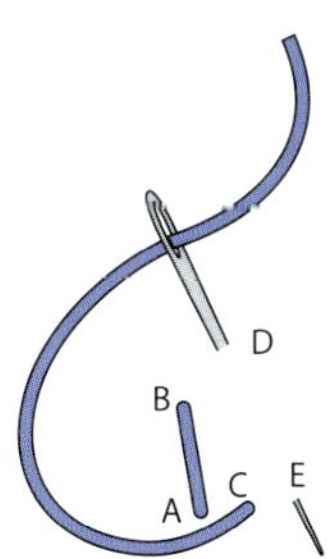

2. Stitch in at D to create a new stitch. Exit at E to start another stitch.

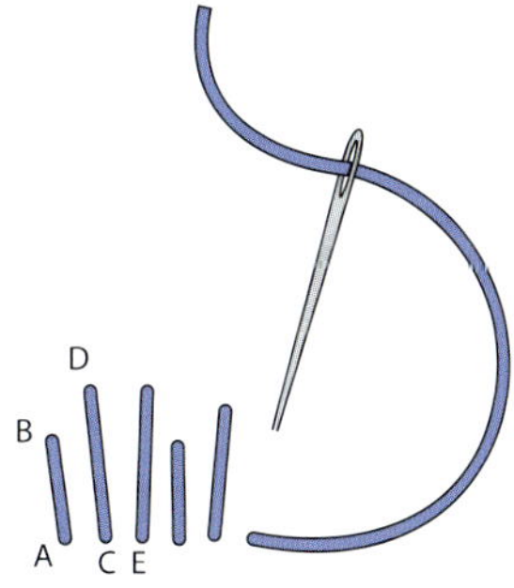

3. Make as many stitches as necessary and finish the last stitch.

The cost-saving straight stitch

This stitch saves thread when stitches are large and aligned, by stitching as close as possible to the previous stitch.

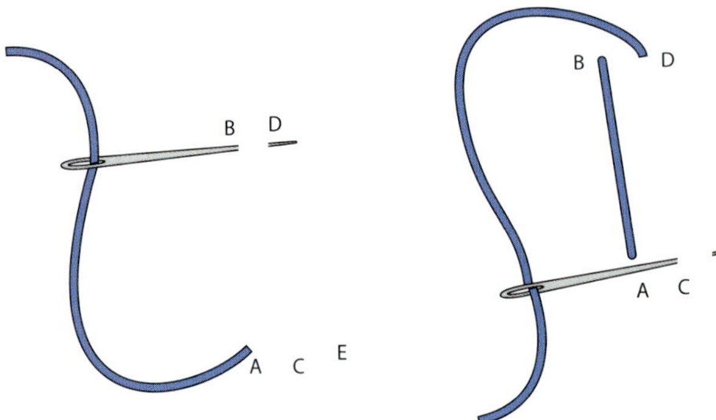

1. Repeat Step 1 for the straight stitch, but this time, exit at D.

2. Stitch at C and exit at E.

The sheaf stitch

The shape resembles a sheaf of wheat.

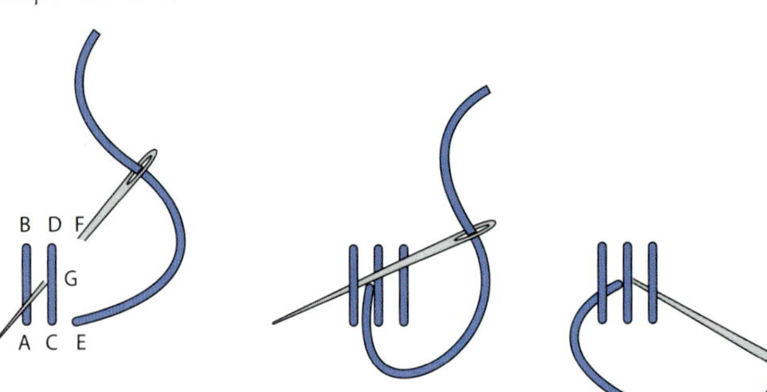

1. Embroider three fairly tight, vertical, long stitches. As you finish the third stitch, pull the needle out to the left of the midpoint of the second stitch (at G).

2. Slide the needle under the first stitch from right to left, without stitching into the fabric.

3. Pass over the three stitches. Slide the needle under the third stitch and stitch to the right of the middle of the second stitch.

4. Pull on the thread to tighten the stitches.

The double rice stitch

This is a long stitch with very small lines. When multiplied, it serves as a filling stitch.

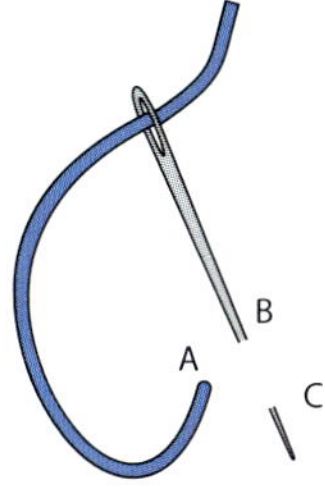

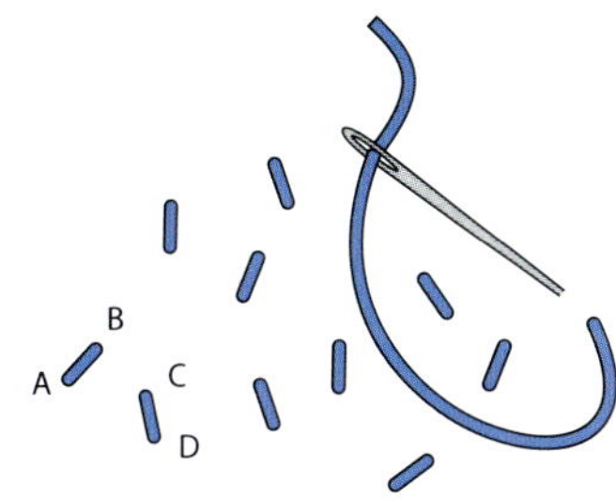

1. Pull the needle out at A. Stitch at B and exit at the point of the new stitch, here at C.
2. Space the dots evenly.

For more depth, this stitch can be doubled.

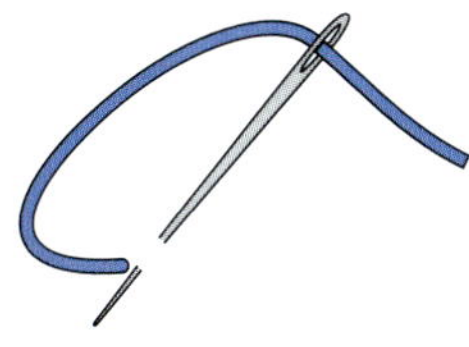

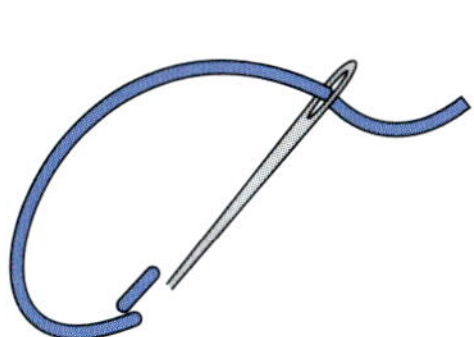

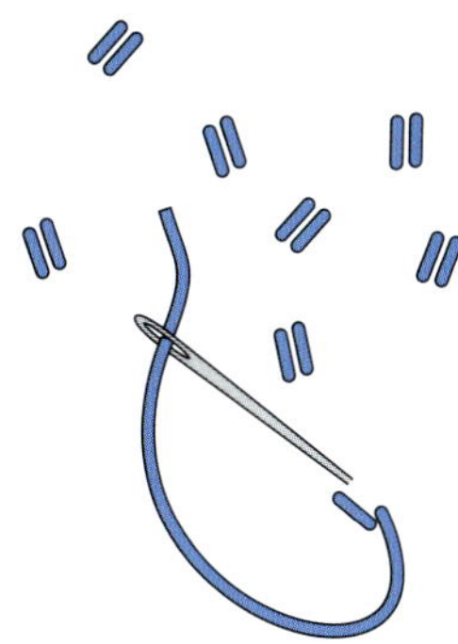

1. Make a stitch.
2. Make a second stitch right next to it, the same size as and parallel to the first.
3. Pull the needle out farther to continue.

The cross stitch (and variations)

Cross stitch is ideal for filling in designs called "grids." You can embroider it alone as a design (for example, to make noses for stuffed animals), or side by side to fill a grid. Before starting, draw a square or just mark its four corners.

The single cross stitch

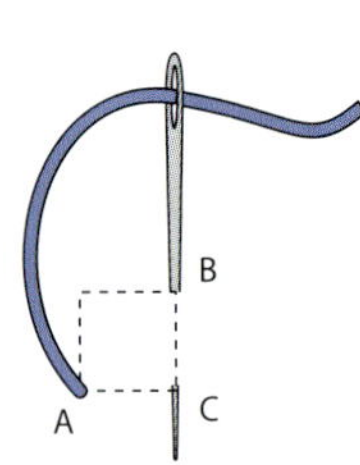

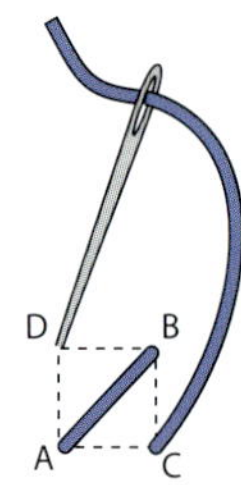

1. Pull the needle out at A. Stitch in the opposite corner at B. Pull out vertically at C.
2. Finish by stitching in at D, vertically to A. Both stitches are oblique.

> **TIP**
>
> **Mark the stitches by enlarging the holes with your needles.**

The straight cross stitch

The cross is embroidered in the opposite direction. One stitch is vertical, the other horizontal.

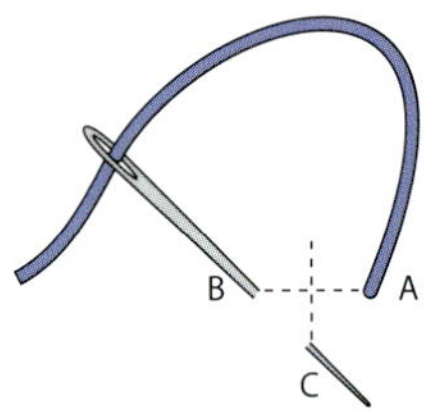

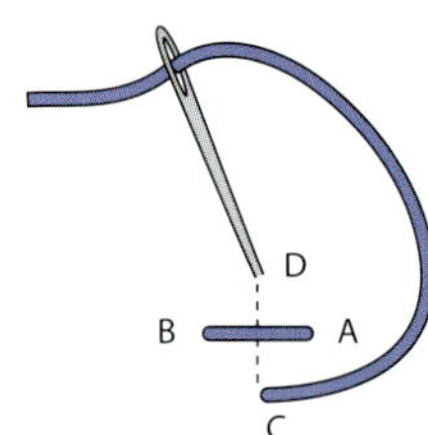

1. Make a horizontal stitch from A to B and pull the needle out at C.
2. End with a vertical stitch at D.

The double cross stitch

Embroider a single cross stitch and a straight cross stitch on the same basic square.

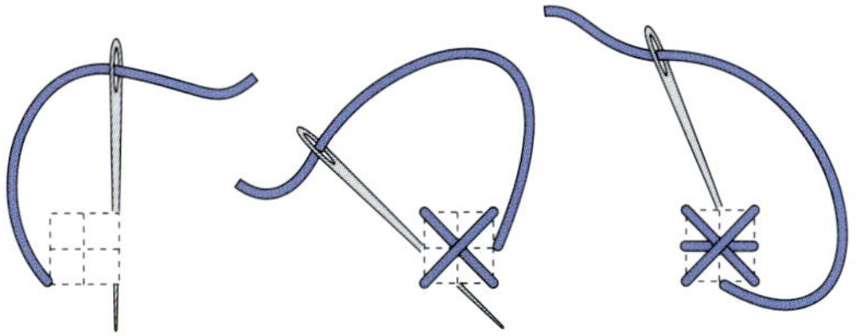

> **NOTE**
>
> **When embroidering several stitches, make sure to follow the steps carefully so that the threads are always in the same direction. This rule goes for all stitches.**

The star stitch

These are straight stitches that start from the center. To help you, draw a circle with a compass.

The eight-pointed star

To space the branches of this star evenly, first embroider them crosswise, face to face, then make the intermediate stitches.

To form a cross, stitch horizontally, then vertically.

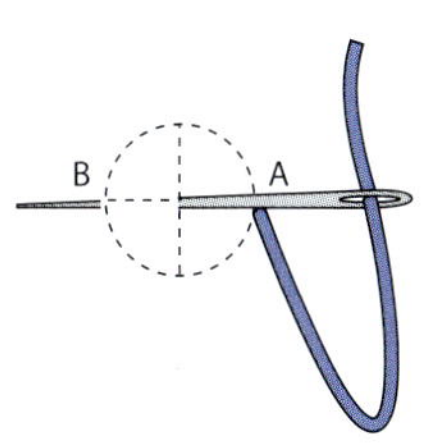

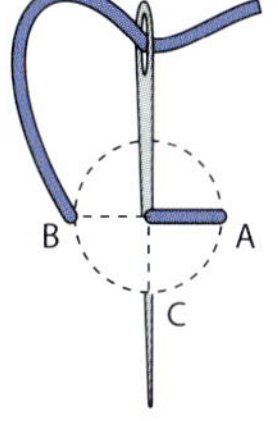

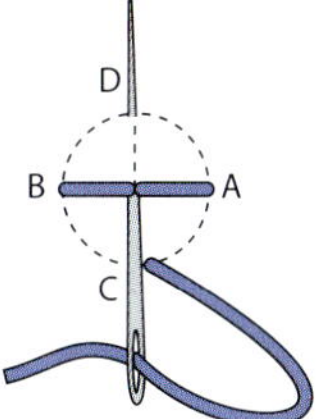

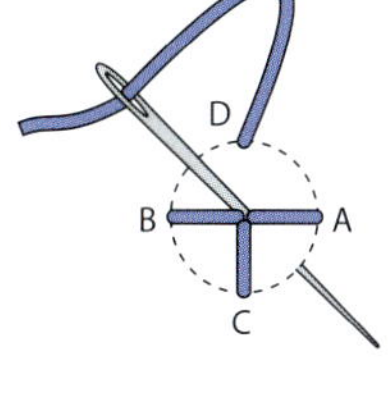

1. Pull the needle out to the right at A. Stitch in the center and exit to the left at B.
2. Stitch in the center and exit at the bottom at C.
3. Stitch in the center and exit at the top at D.
4. Stitch in the center and exit at E (in the middle of AC).

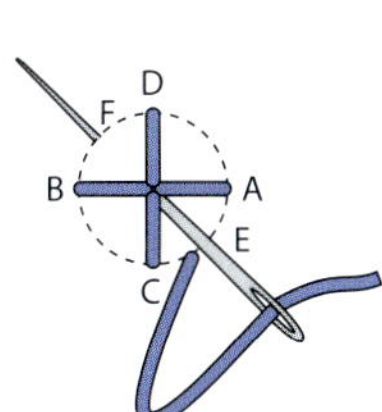

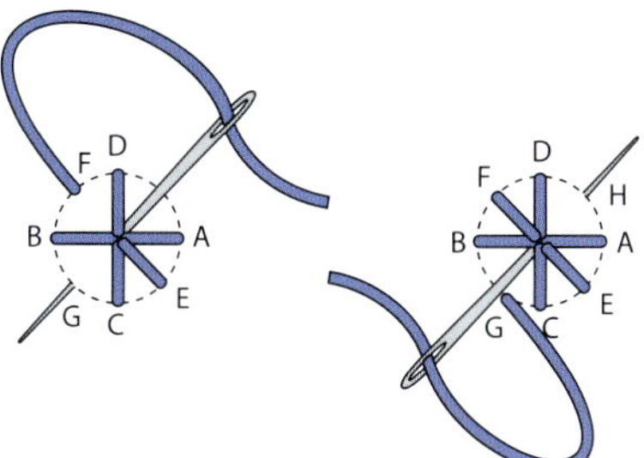

5. Continue by embroidering between the completed stitches.

6. Finish by stitching in the center.

The five-pointed star

For the five-pointed star, embroider the stitches one after the other.

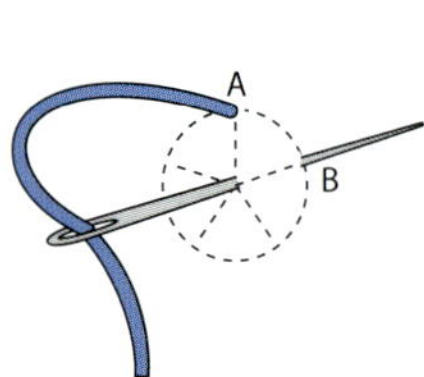

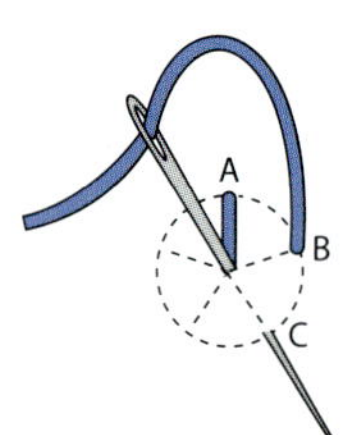

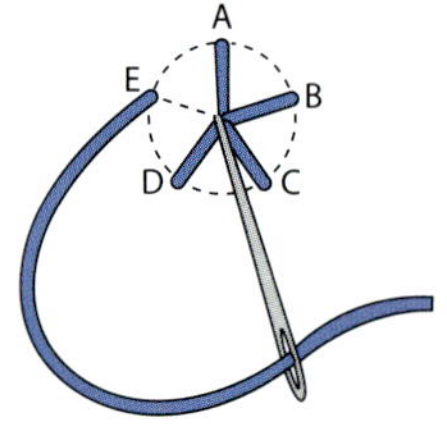

1. Take out the thread at A. Stitch in the center and take out at B.
2. Stitch in the center and exit at C. Continue until you reach E.
3. Finish by stitching in the center.

The web stitch

With the web stitch, you can embroider circles or suns.

First make a star stitch with an odd number of branches.

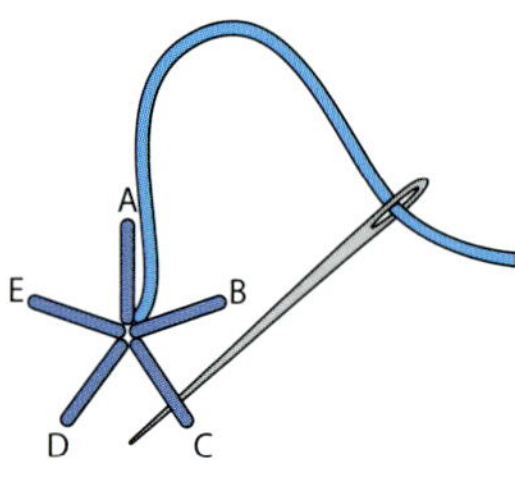

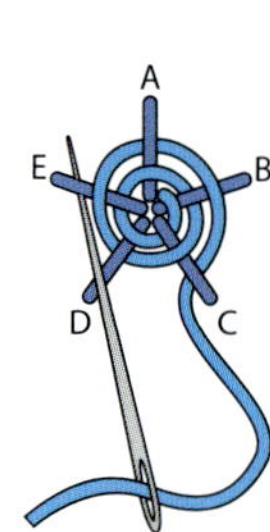

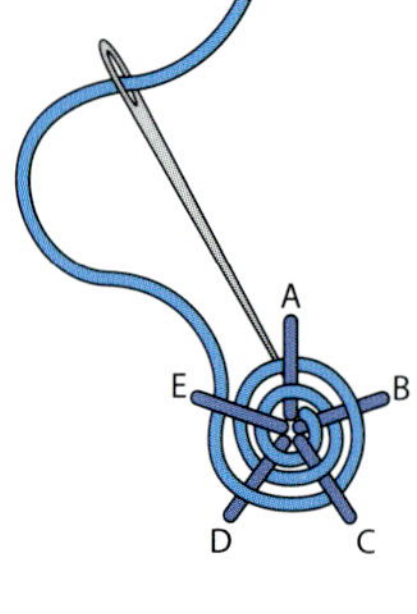

1. Pull the needle out between AB.
2. Continue by stitching alternatively, above and below the threads. Go over B and under C.
3. Finish by stitching under a strand.

The fern stitch

The fern stitch resembles the fronds of a fern. It is embroidered from top to bottom.

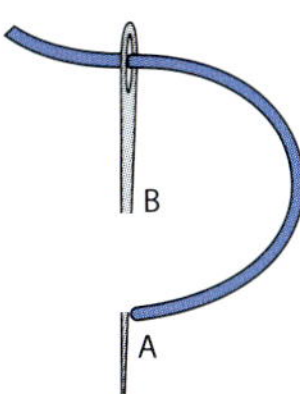

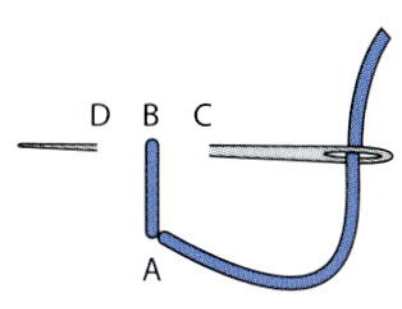

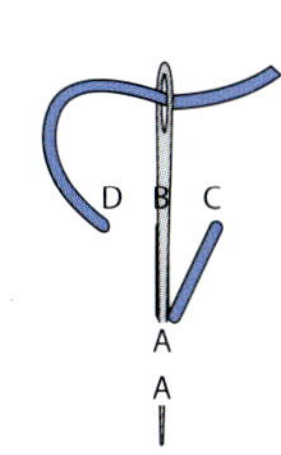

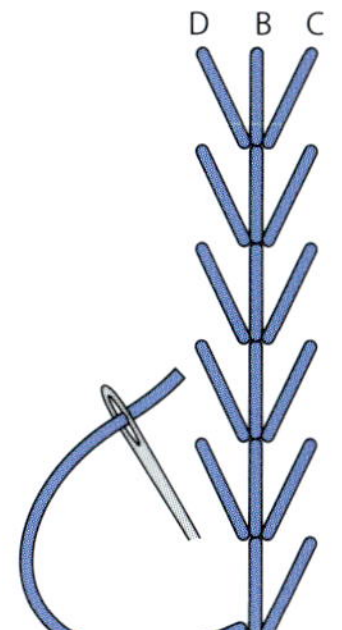

1. Pull needle out at A. Stitch over at B and pull out at A.
2. Stitch in at C to the right of B and exit at D to the left of B—B is in the middle of CD.
3. Stitch at A and pull out underneath to make a new stitch.
4. Continue in this way from top to bottom. Finish with the last stitch.

The single fly stitch

The single fly stitch looks like a V or a Y, depending on the length of its vertical thread. It is embroidered from left to right.

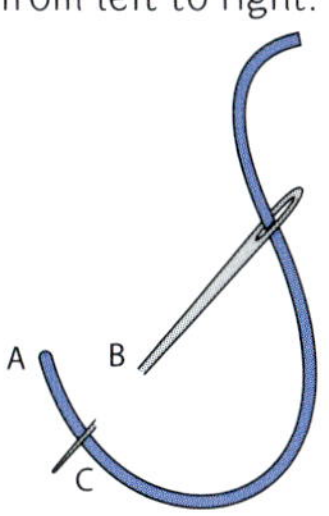

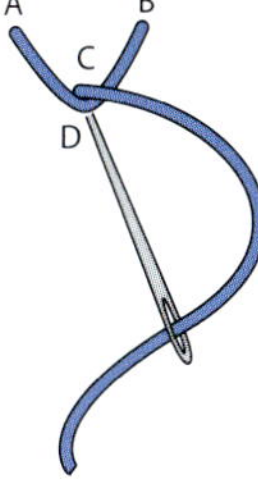

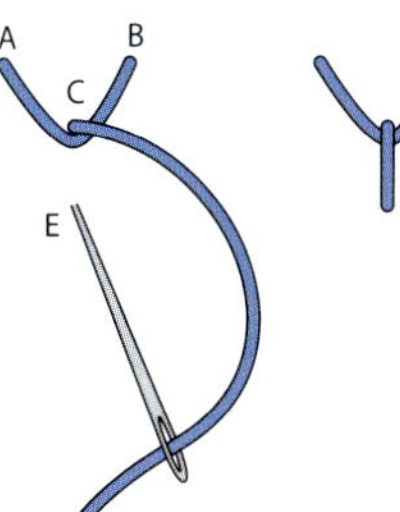

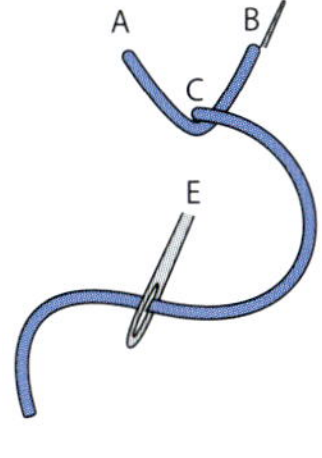

1. Pull the needle out at A. Stitch at B and exit at C, passing the thread under the point.
2. Stitch at D just below the thread to secure the stitch. You'll get a V shape.
3. To embroider a Y, finish lower at E.
4. For loops or curls, embroider from left to right. Make a V or Y and pull the needle out to B for the next stitch.

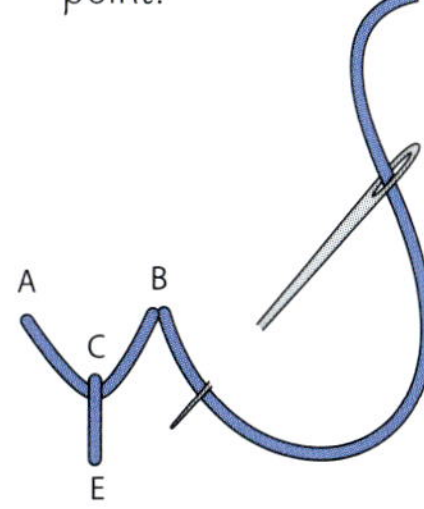

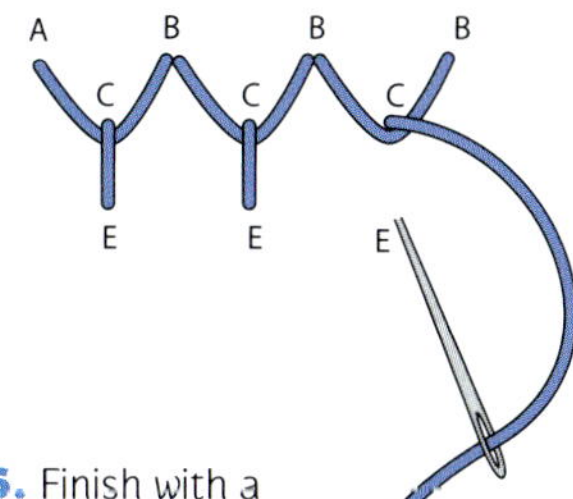

5. Continue to the side.
6. Finish with a vertical stitch.

TIP

To make several stitches, embroider them from left to right, then from right to left for the bottom line.

The lazy daisy stitch

The lazy daisy stitch allows you to draw small flowers. It can be embroidered alone or in groups. Draw a circle with the compass and two lines in cross stitch.

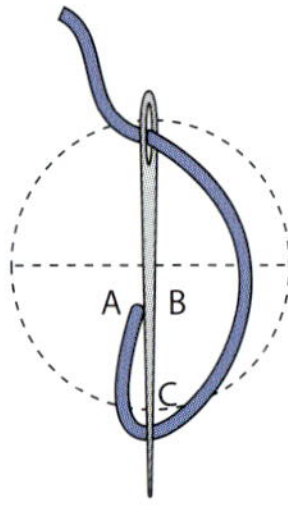

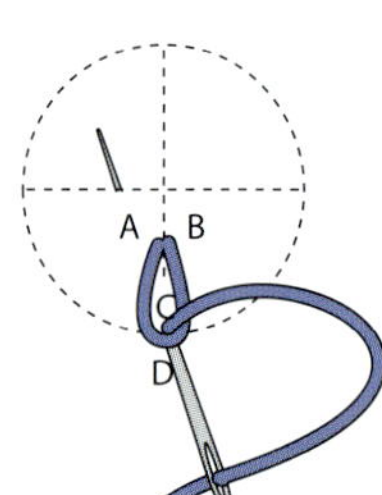

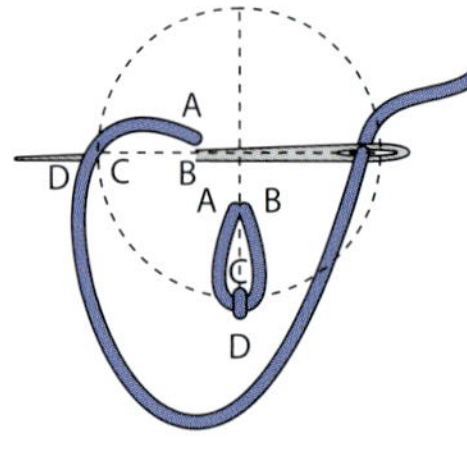

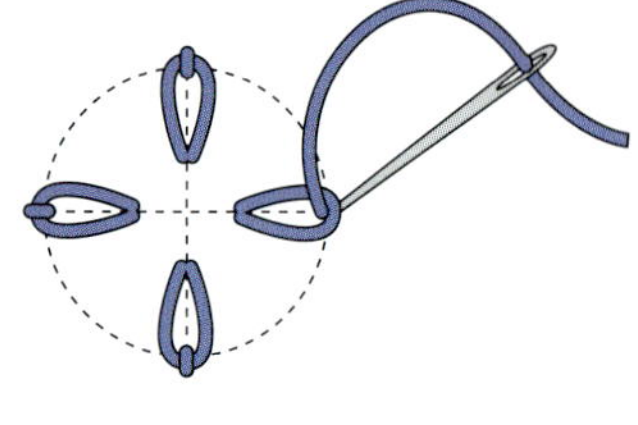

1. Pull the needle out at A on the vertical line. Stitch through the same hole, making a loop, and exit at C on the circle, passing the thread under the point. Don't pull too hard on the loop.
2. Secure the loop by stitching just below the D-thread. To embroider a new stitch, pull the thread out on the following line.
3. Continue by embroidering a loop on each line, following the circle.
4. Finish by fastening the last loop.

The French knot

With the French knot, you can embroider items such as eyes and snowflakes.

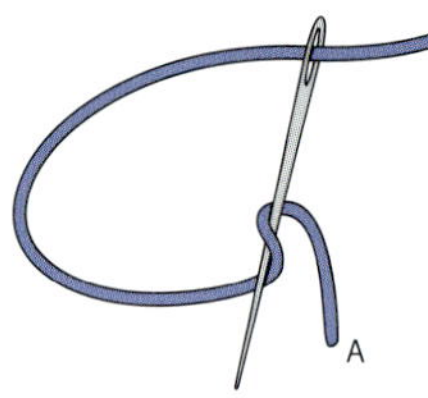

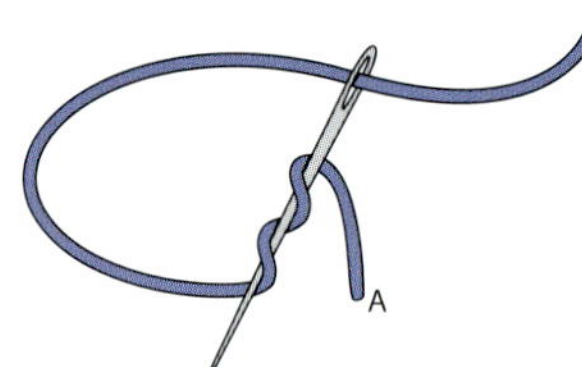

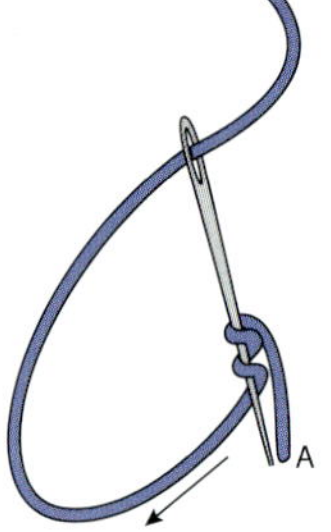

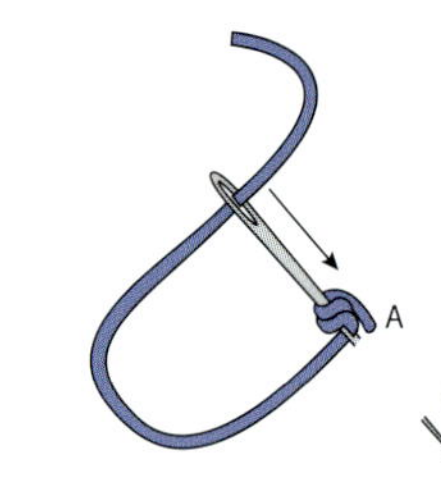

1. Pull the needle out at A and wrap the thread twice around it. If the thread is thick, once is enough.
2. Stitch next to or in the same hole and pull the thread gently toward the fabric.
3. Continue to pull on the thread and push the needle in to close the knot. To embroider another stitch, pull it out farther.
4. If you want to fill a shape, make a pattern of regularly repeated stitches. Finish with step 3, but without removing the needle.

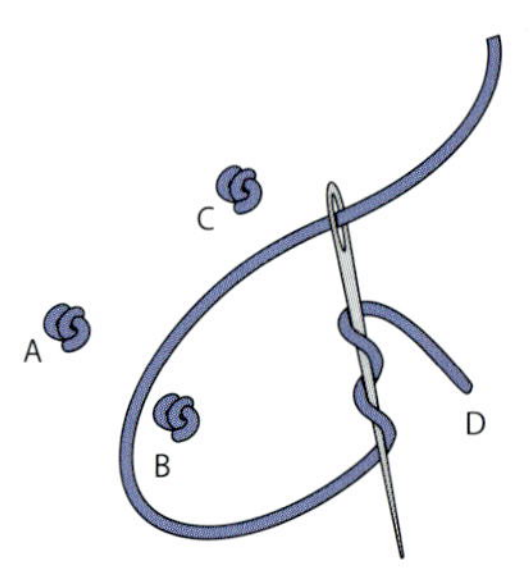

TO CREATE BORDERS

By repeating these stitches, you can create friezes or borders.

The blanket stitch

The blanket stitch is often used to border knitwear or to sew appliqués (fabric designs).

It is embroidered from left to right.

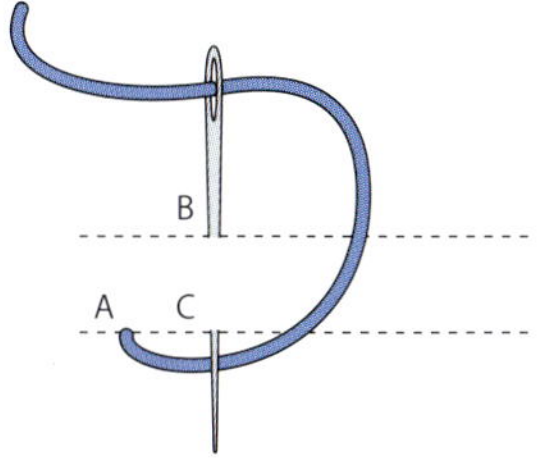

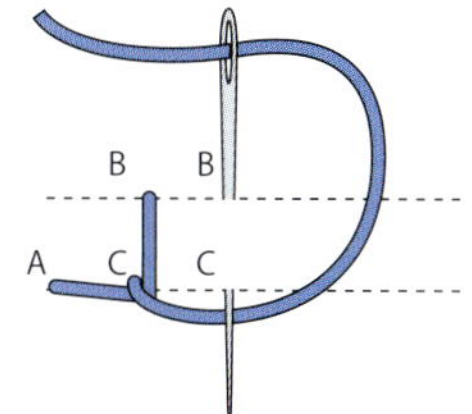

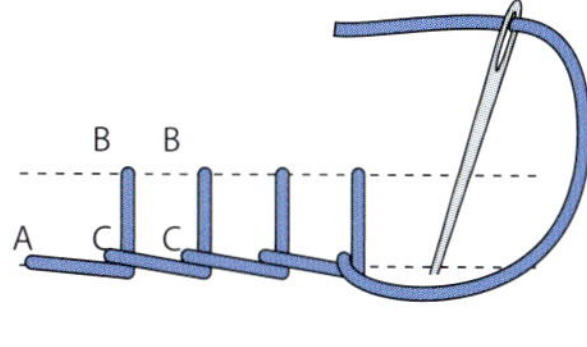

1. Draw two horizontal lines.
2. Pull the needle out at A on the bottom line. Stitch at B on the top line and exit at C vertically on the bottom line, passing the thread under the stitch.
3. Continue with stitches of the same width.
4. Finish with a small stitch right next to the last stitch to secure it.

The buttonhole stitch

The buttonhole stitch is used for buttonholes. It is made in the same way as the blanket stitch, but the stitches must be close together.

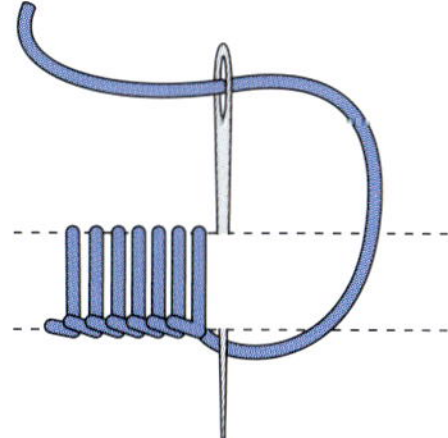

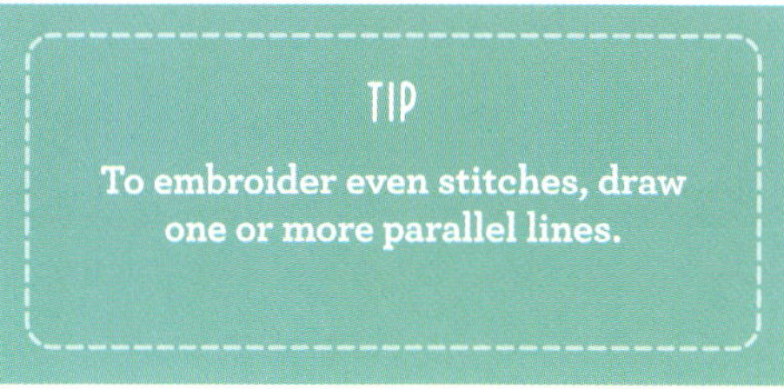

TIP

To embroider even stitches, draw one or more parallel lines.

The feather stitch

The feather stitch is very decorative. You can draw flower stems or create appliqués. Embroider from top to bottom.

The straight feather stitch

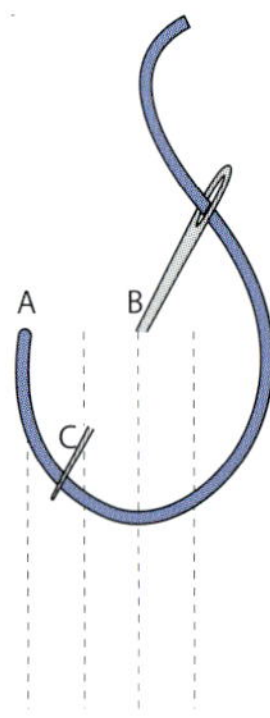

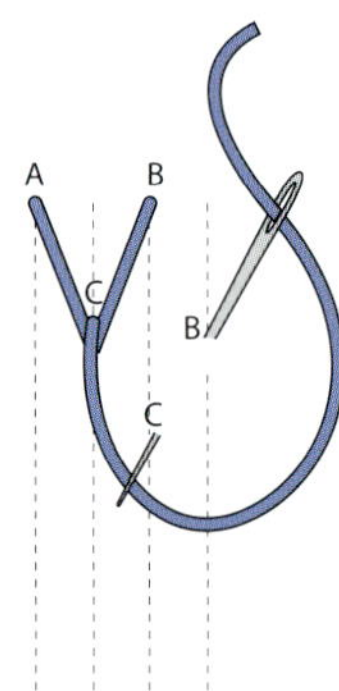

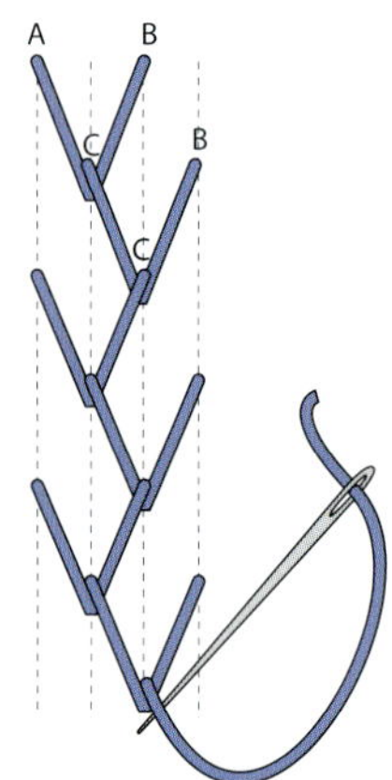

1. Draw four vertical lines. The width of a point is defined by the space between three lines.
2. Pull the needle out at A on the first row. Stitch at the same height on the third line at B and pull out lower at C on the second line, passing the thread under the tip.
3. Repeat, shifting one line to the right.
4. Continue, alternating stitches left and right.
5. To finish, secure the last stitch by stitching just below the thread.

The oblique feather stitch

The oblique feather stitch is embroidered along two vertical lines. The width of a stitch is defined by the space between two lines.

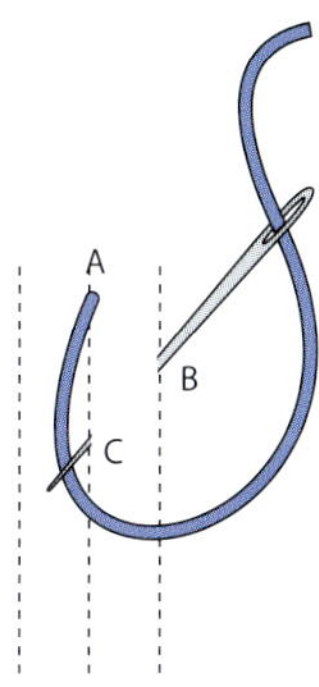

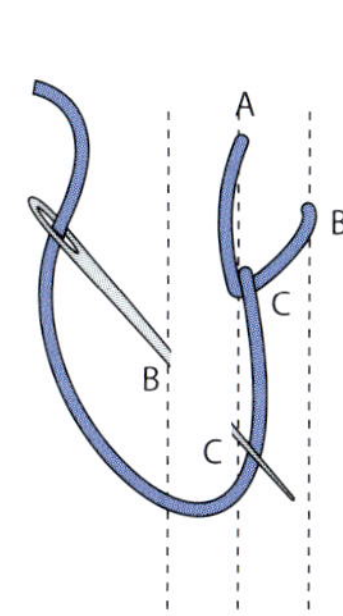

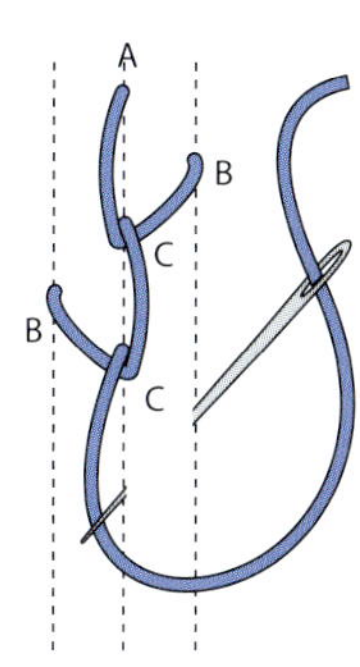

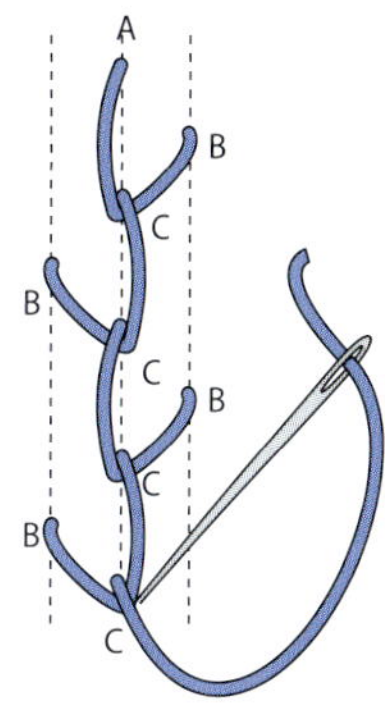

1. Pull the needle out to the middle line at A. Stitch lower on the right-hand line at B and pull out lower at C under A, passing the thread under the tip.

2. Repeat on the left-hand line, lower down.

3. Continue, alternating stitches left and right.

4. Finally, fix the last stitch by stitching just under the thread.

The double feather stitch

The double feather stitch produces a zigzag effect.

1. Embroider a straight feather stitch, alternating two stitches to the right and two to the left.
2. Secure the last stitch by stitching just under the thread.

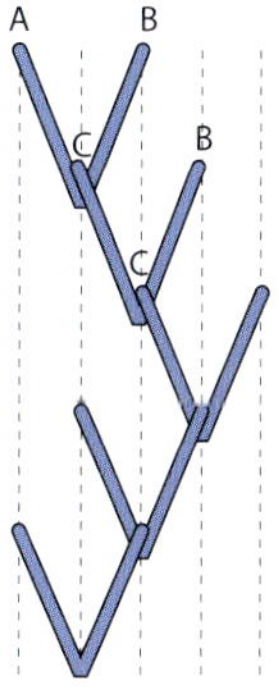

The Persian or plaited stitch

The Persian or plaited stitch is embroidered from left to right.

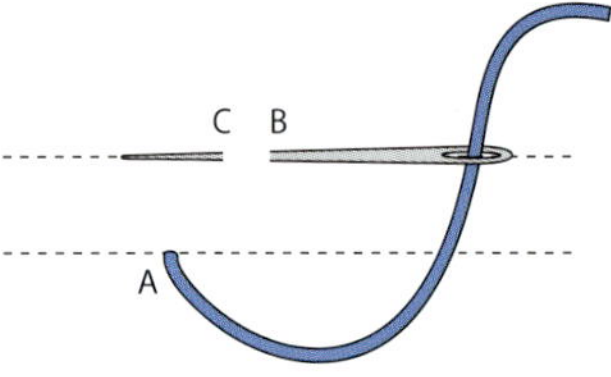

1. Draw two horizontal lines.

2. Pull the needle out on the bottom line at A. Stitch at B on the top line and pull back at C.

3. Stitch at D on the bottom line and back out at E.

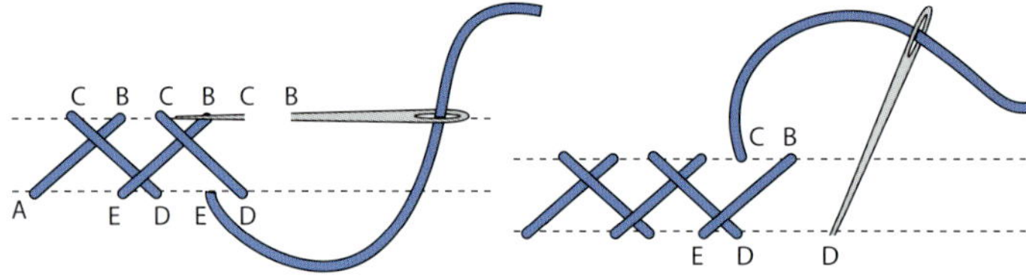

4. Repeat steps 2 and 3. The spaces must be even.

5. Finish at D.

FILLING STITCHES

These stitches can be used to fill in designs that have already been drawn with linear points

The darning stitch

The darning stitch can be quickly embroidered and can be embroidered in both directions.

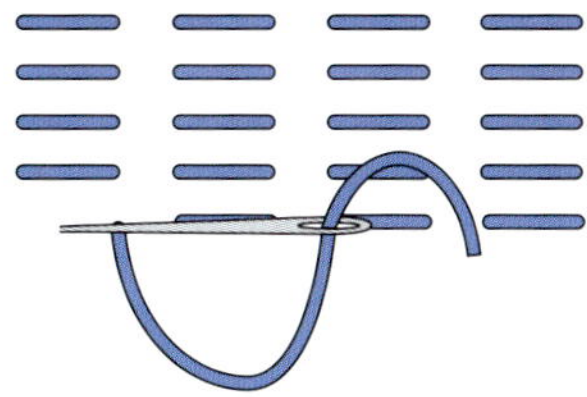

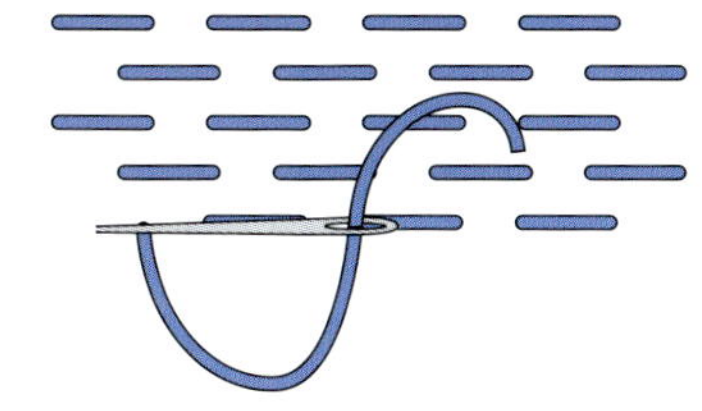

1. Draw horizontal lines or follow the lines on the fabric if they are clearly visible.

2. Embroider lines in front stitch by aligning the stitches or staggering them.

The long-armed cross stitch

Unlike cross stitch (see page 44), this stitch is embroidered in groups, from left to right.

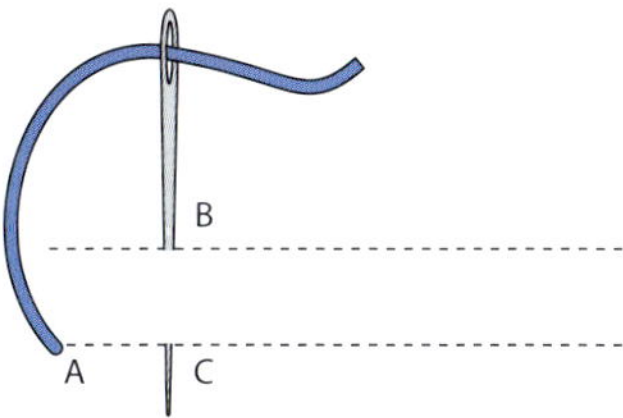

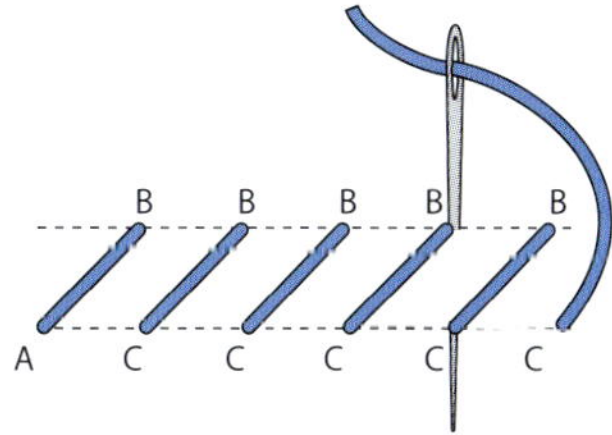

1. Draw horizontal lines.

2. Pull the needle out at A, on the bottom line. Stitch on the top line at B, on the right, and exit underneath vertically at C.

3. Embroider a series of oblique stitches at the same angle. After the last stitch, pull out the needle at C.

4. Stitch the needle obliquely in the other direction and pull it out from underneath.

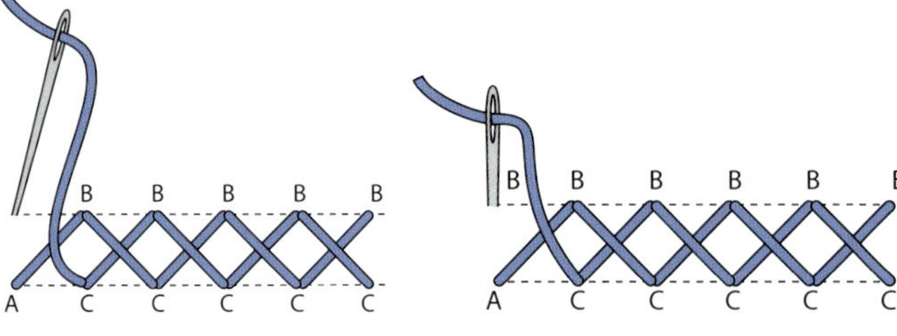

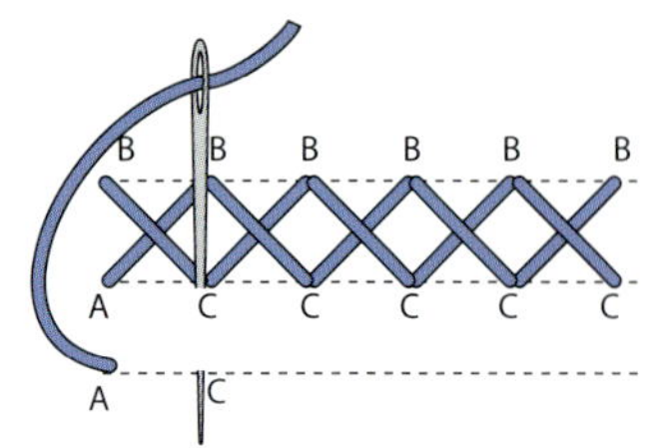

5. Embroider a series of stitches from right to left, over the others, stitching in the same holes.

6. To embroider a new line, draw a line underneath. Pull the needle out on this line at A.

7. Repeat Step 2, stitching in the holes.

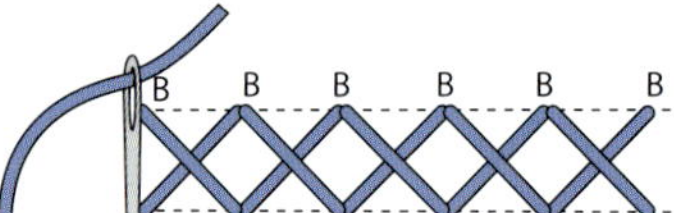

8. Go back and forth again. Embroider another line underneath.

The half cross stitch

This is a half cross stitch.

1. Repeat the cross stitch Steps 1 to 3.

2. Draw a line underneath and stitch the half stitches backward, from right to left.

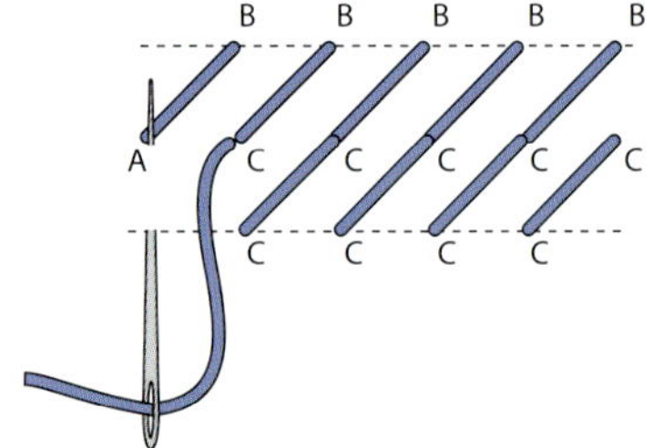

The reversible cross stitch

This involves embroidering every other stitch and then the other stitches in a new pass to avoid vertical stitches on the reverse side.

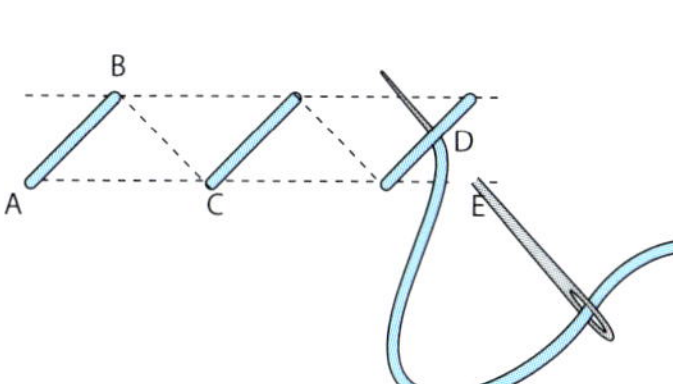

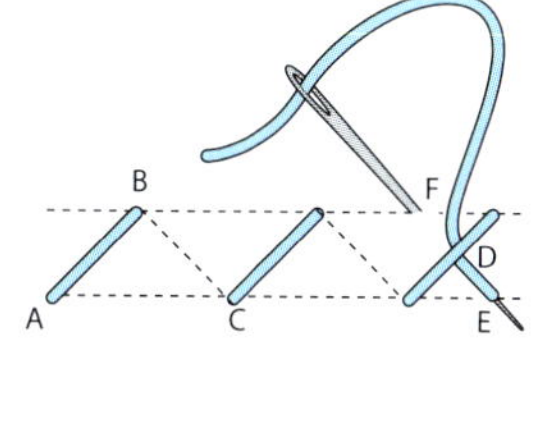

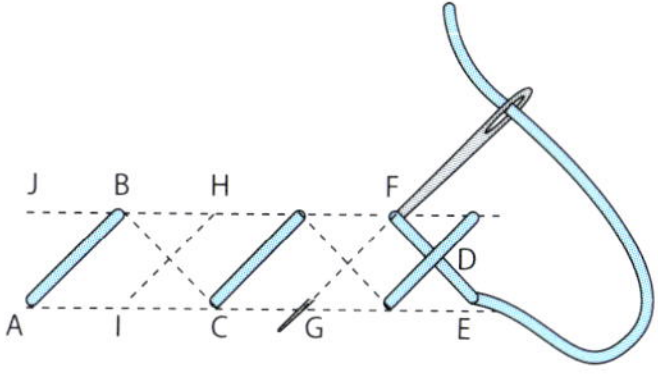

1. Pull the needle out at A. Stitch at B and pull out at C. Repeat until the end of the row. Take out at D (in the middle of the last stitch), stitch at E, and take out again at D (in the middle of the last stitch).

2. Stitch at F to complete the stitch and exit at E.

3. Stitch again at F and exit at G. The last stitch is double.

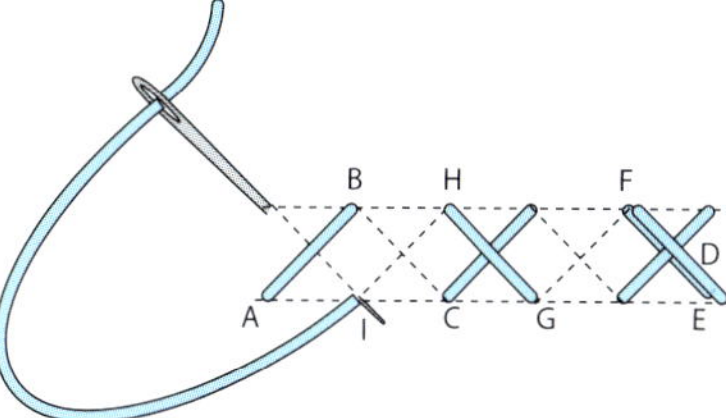

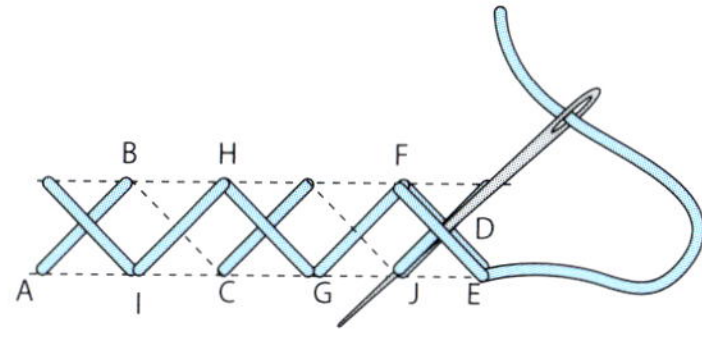

4. Stitch at H, exit at I, and finish the last stitch. Exit again at I. You've embroidered one of two crosses.

5. Stitch at H, exit at G. Repeat to the end of the row. Exit at E, stitch at D, and exit at J.

6. Finish the intermediate crosses.

7. On the reverse side, hide the threads under the stitches.

The satin stitch (and variations)

The satin stitch is used for needlepoint, since it can fill in small areas. It is embroidered from left to right.

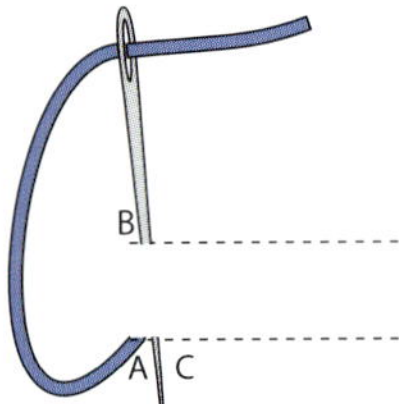

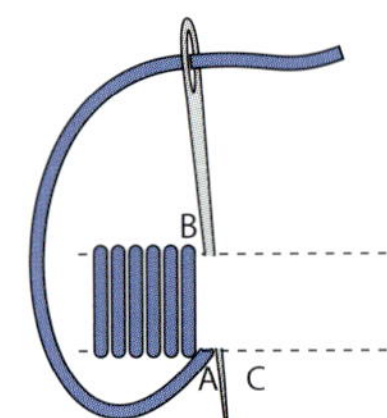

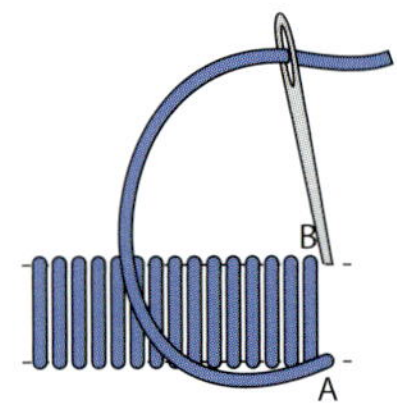

1. Pull the needle out at A on the bottom line. Stitch at B, vertically, and pull out underneath at C, right next to the thread.
2. Embroider a series of tight vertical stitches. Don't pull too hard on the thread; the tension should be even.
3. Finish at the top.

The double satin stitch

The double satin stitch hides the junction between the first and second rows of embroidery. Stitches in the same row are the same size.

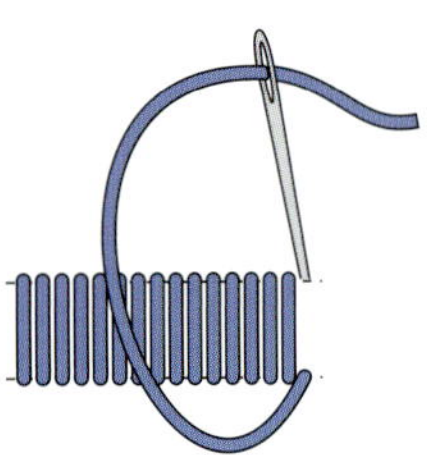

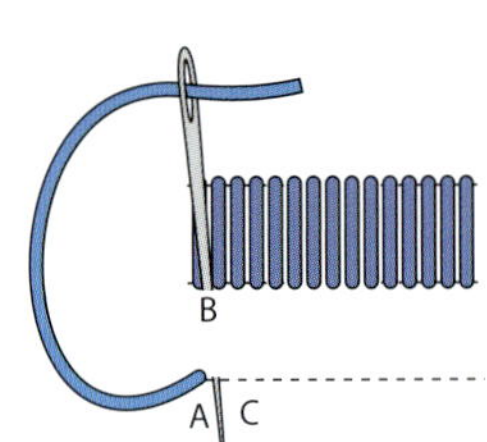

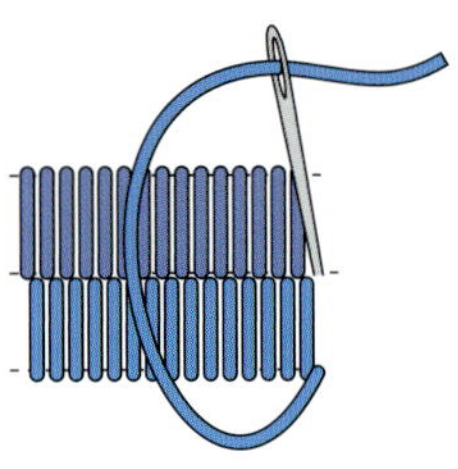

1. Make a line with a satin stitch.
2. To embroider the second line, take a new thread (of the same or a different color). Pull out the needle at A, between the two top stitches. Stitch at B, between the two stitches, and exit next to the thread, between the next two stitches.
3. Embroider a new series of stitches underneath, staggering them: Each stitch underneath is between each stitch above.

The brick stitch

This technique gives you a great deal of freedom. Stitches can be of different lengths and inclinations as long as they fill the surface. It is embroidered from left to right.

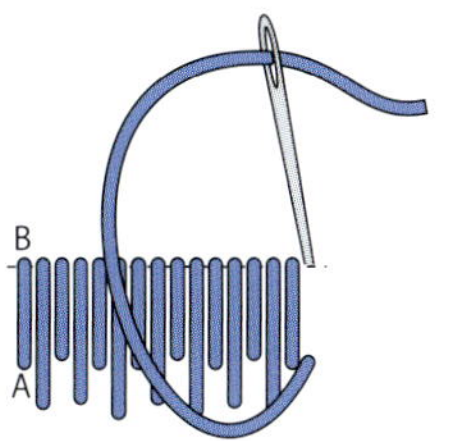

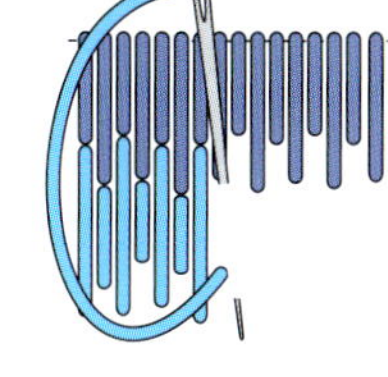

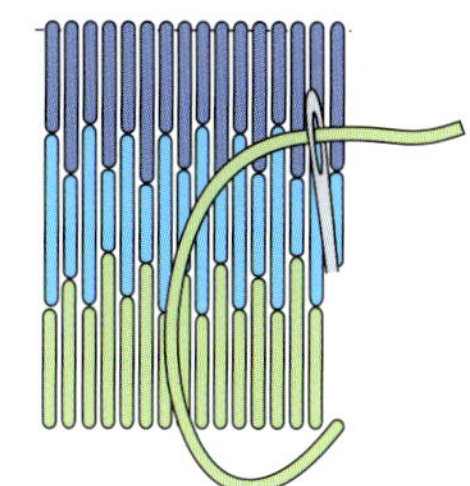

1. Pull the needle out at A and alternate long and short stitches.
2. In the next row, line the stitches up below those above.
3. The stitches interlock, and the boundary is hidden.

The lattice stitch

The lattice stitch is a succession of horizontal and vertical stitches. Draw a grid or count the threads to get your bearings.

1. Trace the outline of the shape to be filled in with a pencil or erasable marker, and embroider it with a straight stitch.
2. Draw a grid inside the outline or count the threads to find your way around.

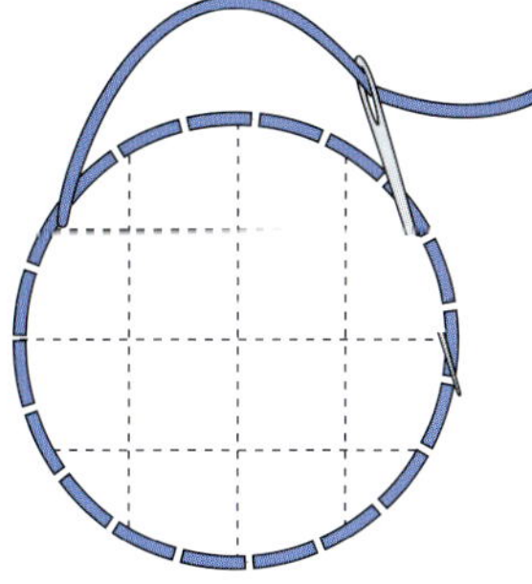

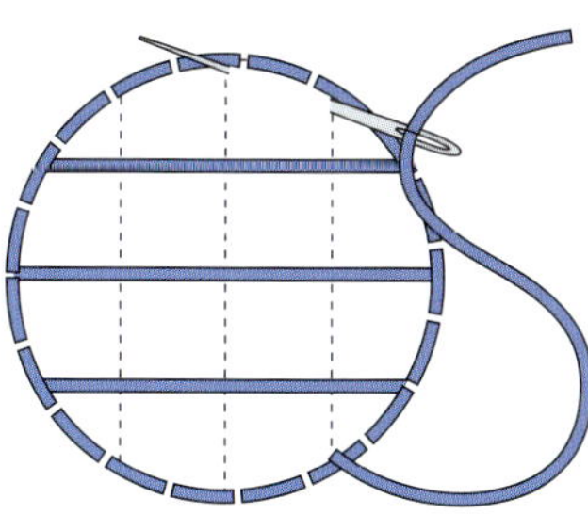

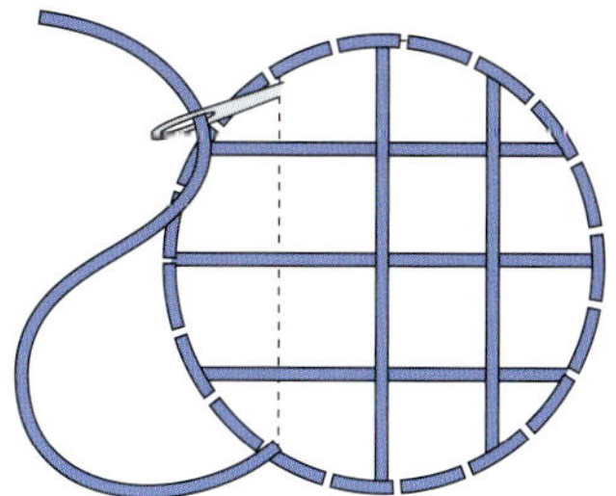

3. Stitch the horizontal lines of the grid, starting and stopping the stitches on the outline of the shape you wish to fill.
4. Embroider the vertical lines.

FINISHING TOUCHES

Once your embroidery has been completed, a few finishing touches are essential to ensure that it looks its best and doesn't fade over time.

Before proceeding with these steps, you need to remove your embroidery from the hoop. To do this, simply loosen the screw and press on the inner ring of the hoop to release the fabric. Be careful not to pull the cloth between the rings, since this may deform it.

WASHING

Check the label to ensure that the fabric or garment on which you'll be embroidering is machine- or hand-washable. Commercial embroidery fabrics are usually 100% linen or cotton and may shrink slightly. It is therefore advisable to wash them before embroidering (see page 23).

If you have embroidered a garment or soiled your embroidery while working, clean the work by hand or machine, following the washing instructions for the fabric or canvas. When machine washing, protect your work by placing it in a fabric pouch or laundry net.

> **NOTE**
>
> **Brand-name embroidery threads won't fade, and the color won't rub off.**

Above all, don't use your washing machine's spin cycle, but roll it in a terry towel to absorb the moisture.

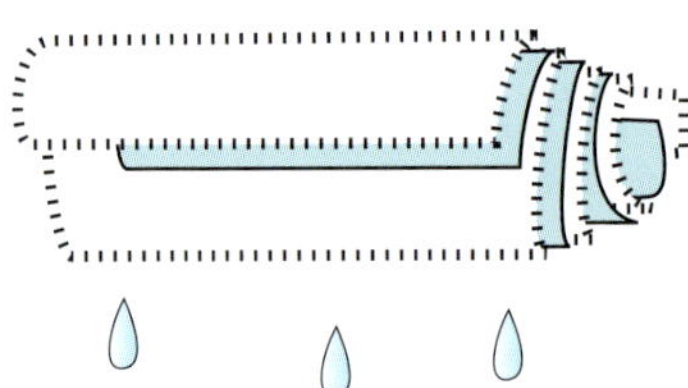

SHAPING

Occasionally, the canvas may become distorted while you're working, especially when you use oblique stitches. In this case, you'll need to shape it. This step should be carried out after washing, but before drying.

1. If you haven't planned to wash your work, simply dampen the fabric by running it under running water or by spraying it.
2. Trace an embroidery frame on a piece of fabric and place it on the ironing board.
3. Gently stretch the corners of your embroidered piece and pin it to the fabric, aligning the outer threads of the piece on the frame.
4. Leave to dry or iron without steam, since the fabric is already damp. If you're ironing, pin the fabric to the reverse first, to avoid crushing the embroidery.

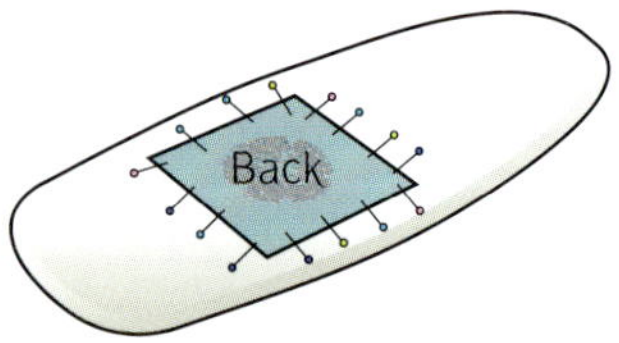

> **STARCH BATH**
>
> ***Embroidery can be starch-treated for extra hold by soaking it in a starch bath. Starch can be bought as flakes to be diluted in a little water or as a spray.***

CREATING NEAT EDGES

When the embroidery has not been completed on a garment or bag, for example, it is essential that the edges of your work are clean. If you need to reshape the embroidery, do so before finishing the edges. Otherwise, iron afterward.

Surfacing

Edges are hand- or machine-overlocked with a zigzag stitch. This is the simplest technique but offers a less clean finish.

Hemming edges

The only difficulty with this technique lies in the corners. Please note that an additional 1.18-inch margin is required all around the embroidery.

1. Fold the edges over twice by 0.39 inches and mark the creases with a fingernail or iron.

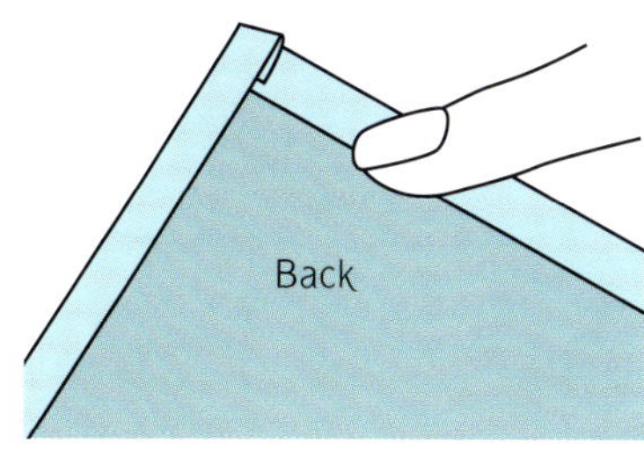

2. Open the folds and cut the corners to loosen them.

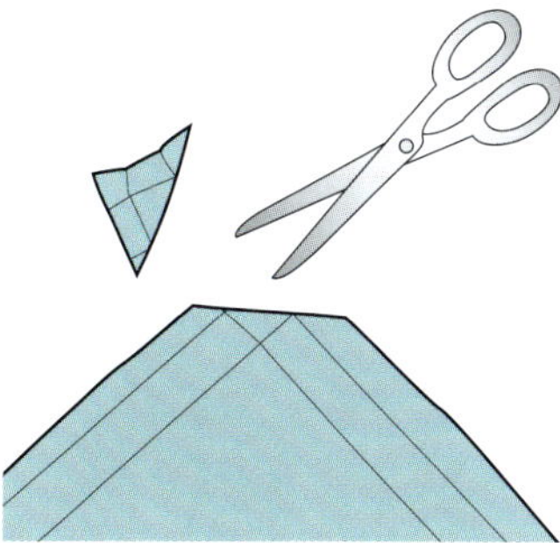

3. Fold the edges over again and hand-stitch with overlock stitch, or machine-stitch 0.19 inches from the edge in straight stitch.

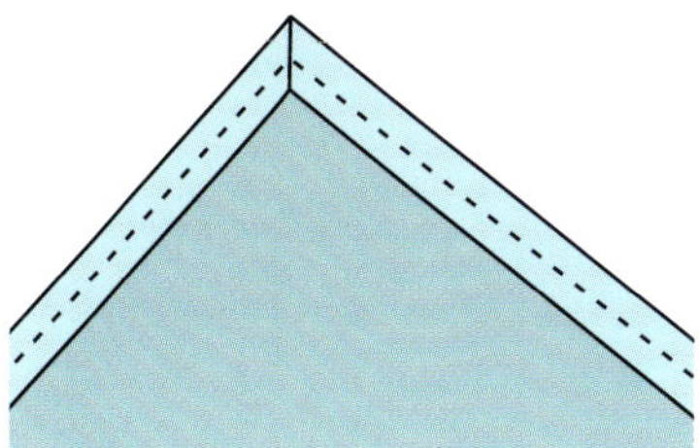

Sewing a bias

Bias finishes off a work of art (e.g., a bib or towel). It's a strip of fabric with each edge folded over. Cut on the diagonal of the fabric. It is elastic, making it perfect for edging rounded shapes. It's best to choose a color that matches the fabric or embroidery.

1. Open the bias. Lay the right sides together against the edge of the fabric. By hand or machine, stitch between the edge and the first fold, 0.07 or 0.11 inches from the first fold. Start stitching 0.2 inches from the end of the bias, folding it in at the end of the seam.

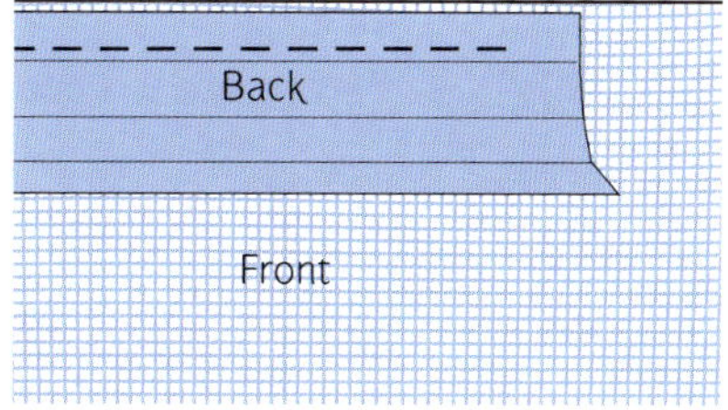

2. In the corners, stretch the bias to turn and cut the corner after sewing.

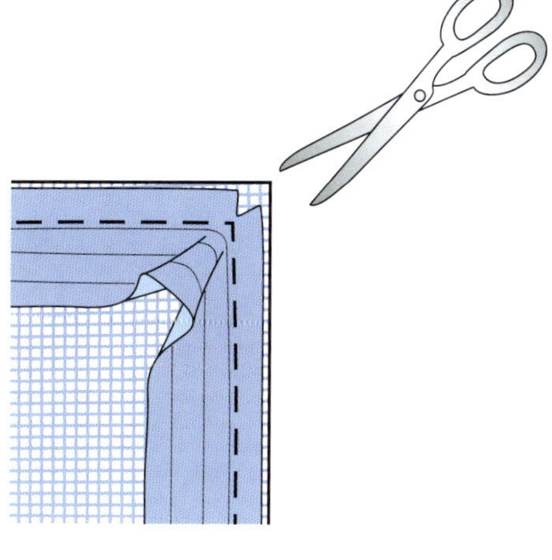

3. To close the turn, fold over the 0.2 inches at the beginning and lay the end of the bias over it. Trim excess bias.

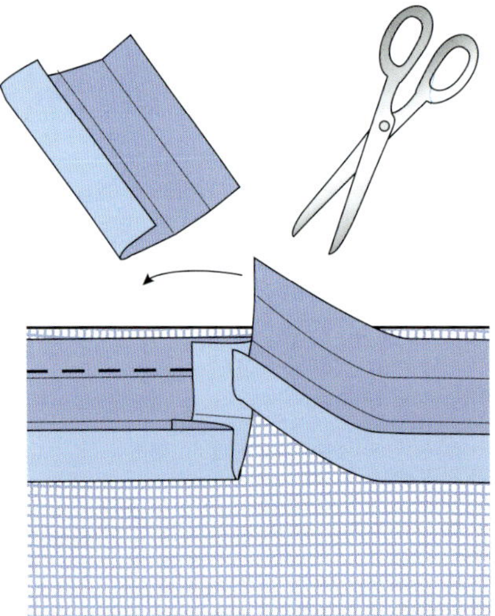

4. Fold the bias binding to the wrong side of the fabric. Hand-sew in overlock stitch.

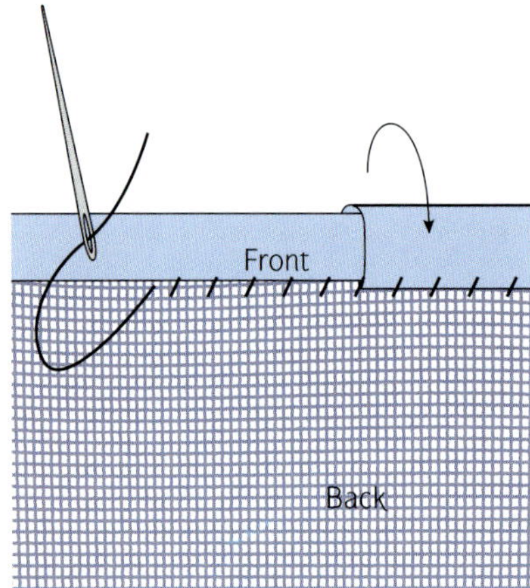

IRONING

If you haven't already done so, iron the embroidery on the reverse side, on a soft surface, so that the stitches retain their depth.

1. Start by making sure your iron is clean. To find out, iron on a white cloth. If it leaves marks, clean it with a cloth soaked in white vinegar and a little salt, and wipe the soleplate with absorbent paper.

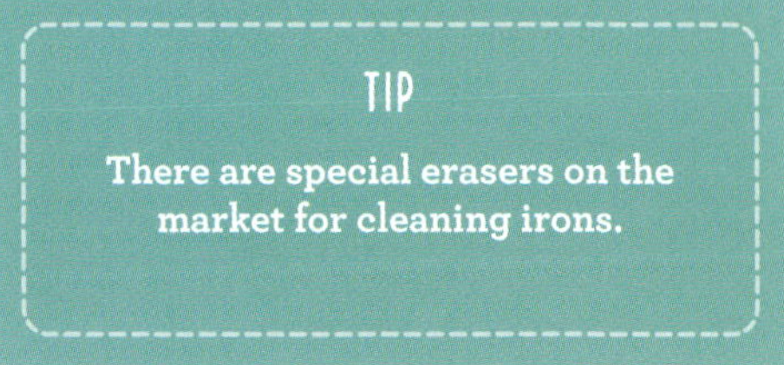

TIP

There are special erasers on the market for cleaning irons.

2. Fold a towel in half on the ironing board.
3. Then place a damp cloth between the embroidery and the iron, or a dry cloth if the embroidery is damp.
4. Iron without steam and with pressure, without going back and forth.

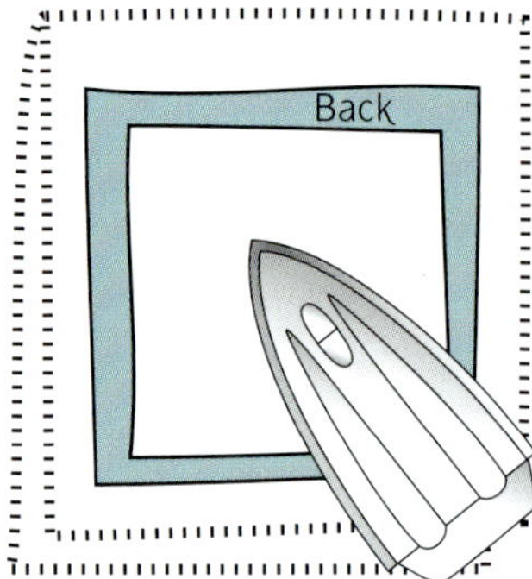

FRAMING

Have fun finding frames at flea markets to personalize your work at low cost! To frame an embroidery, each edge of the work must be 0.2 inches longer than the inside of the frame. The edges don't need to be hemmed, since they won't be visible.

1. Start by removing the glass to prevent moisture from seeping in and causing mold.
2. Cut a thick piece of cardboard to fit the inside of the frame. A cardboard box will do the trick and won't cost you a thing.
3. Cut a piece of felt to the same dimensions and stick it to the cardboard with glue or double-sided tape.

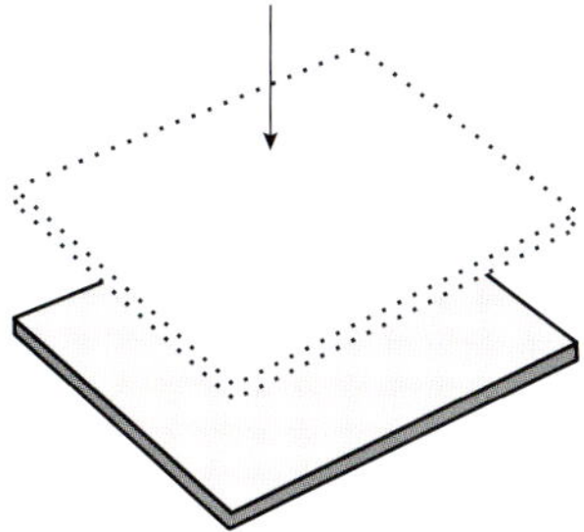

4. Using a pencil, mark the center of each side of the embroidery with a cross, as well as the back of the cardboard. Make sure the markings are on the same thread of the fabric, especially if the weft is thick (such as Aïda canvas, linen, or thick cotton). This prevents the fabric from being placed crookedly, which can be visible.

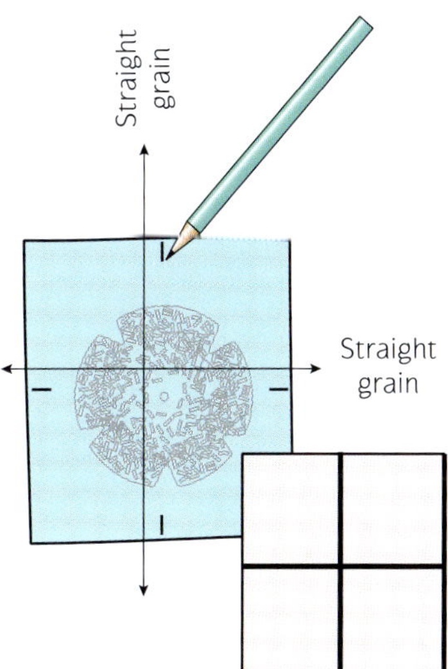

REMINDER

The straight grain runs parallel to the warp threads of the fabric. The fabric doesn't stretch along the straight grain.

5. Center the embroidery on the wadding. Fold the edges over to the back of the cardboard, aligning the marks. Secure them with pins all around by inserting the pins into the cardboard.
6. Remove the pins gradually and glue down the folded edges using a flat brush and fabric glue. If the edges don't align with the grain, pull the corners to adjust them.

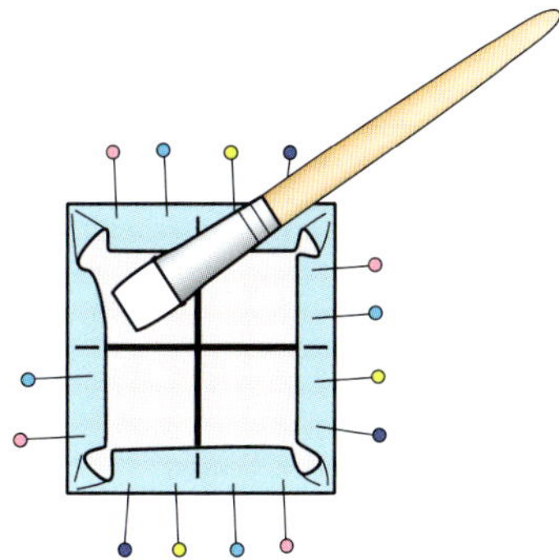

7. Trim the corners and reglue them if necessary.

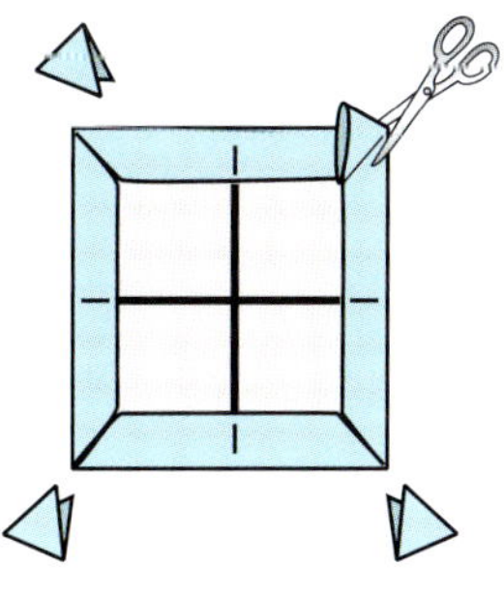

8. Glue a rectangle of paper on the back to hide the folded edges.

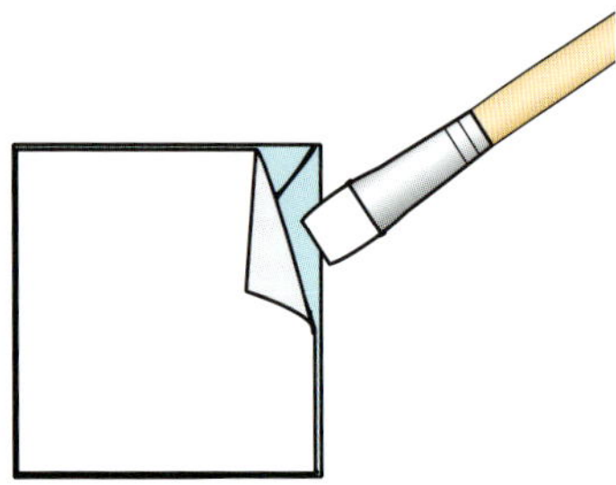

9. Place the assembly in the frame and secure the back of the frame over it.

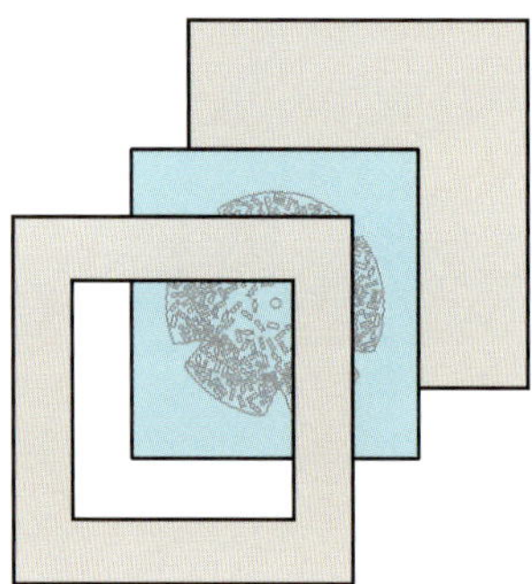

HOOP ART

Hoop art is very trendy. The piece is left in the embroidery hoop, which will be hung on the wall like a frame. In this case, the back of the work should be neat.

1. If needed, remove the embroidery from the hoop and rinse it to remove any marks left by the pen. Then iron it on the reverse side (see page 62).

2. Place the embroidery back in the hoop, ensuring the design is centered and the weave is straight. Tighten the screw securely. Trim the fabric, leaving an 0.8-to-1-inch margin.

3. Fold the fabric over to the back, pulling it tightly, and sew a running stitch 0.4 inches from the edge. Gather the thread tightly to pull the edges toward the center.

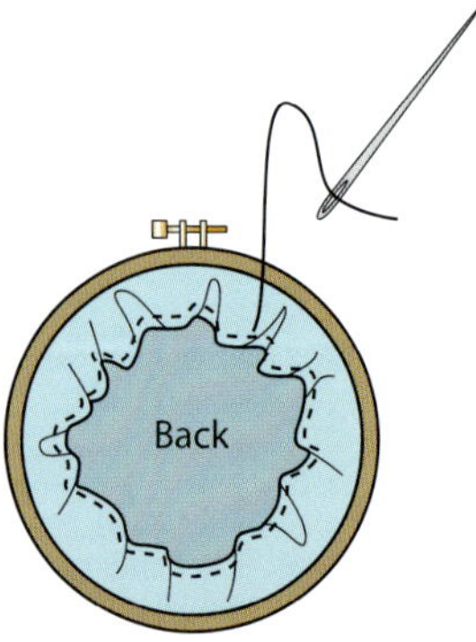

4. Cut a circle of white felt matching the diameter of the inner ring of the hoop. This felt can be replaced with a circle of cardboard or wood, as available commercially.

5. Pin and then sew this felt circle onto the fabric, using an overcast stitch (see page 24).

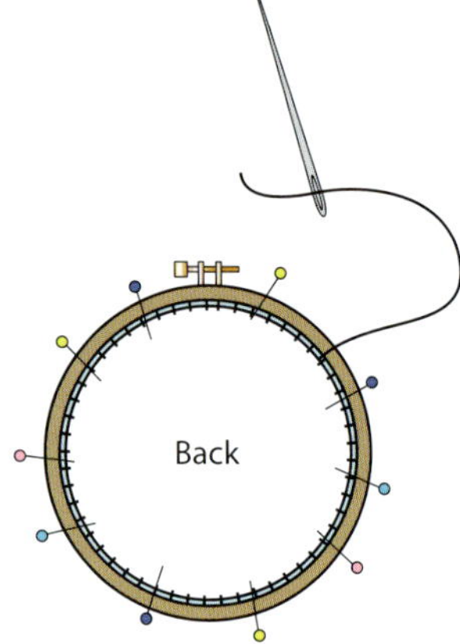

An easier method is to add a layer of fabric before placing the embroidery back in the hoop, and trimming both fabrics close to the edge of the hoop. In this case, add a bit of glue to the outer ring. Choose white fabric if the embroidery is slightly transparent or colored, or a patterned fabric if it is fully opaque.

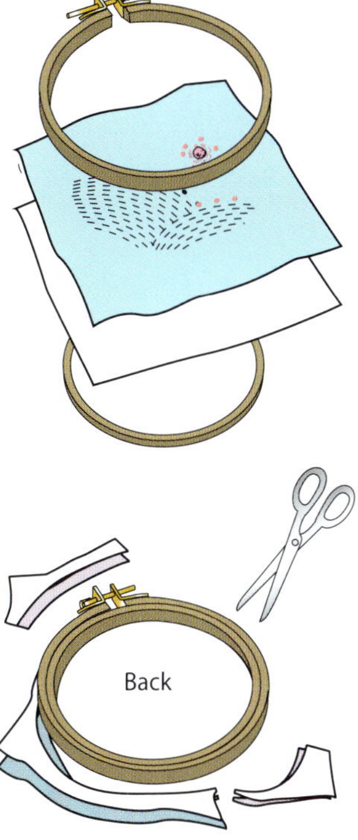

HIDING KNOTS

If you're embroidering on clothing, you'll need to hide any knots on the back. To do this, sew or iron on a piece of fusible interfacing on the back of the embroidery (see page 24).

HIDING A STAIN

Discovered a stain on your embroidery after finishing it? Don't worry! If the fabric is washable, gently clean it by hand and let it dry. If the stain persists, try a commercial stain remover (first test it on a hidden area to avoid any surprises).

If all else fails, as a last resort, embroider a small motif over the stain to conceal it—and give the piece a personal touch!

SPECIAL EMBROIDERY TECHNIQUES

Throughout the ages, many embroidery techniques have been developed that require mastery of basic stitches (see Chapter 3) and their variations. Here, I present the most common techniques that you can master with ease!

RIBBON EMBROIDERY

Ribbon embroidery adds dimension to the piece. It requires knowledge of classic embroidery stitches.

Ribbon embroidery (design by Les Beaux Arts du Fil)

It is typically done with silk, satin, or organza ribbons, available in varying widths from 1 to 3 inches (and even 4 inches for organza, since it is very lightweight and easily gathers).

Instead of purchasing ribbons, you can make your own by cutting strips of printed fabric about 0.4 inches wide. Simply fold them in thirds lengthwise. These homemade ribbons will be stiffer than silk or organza ribbons.

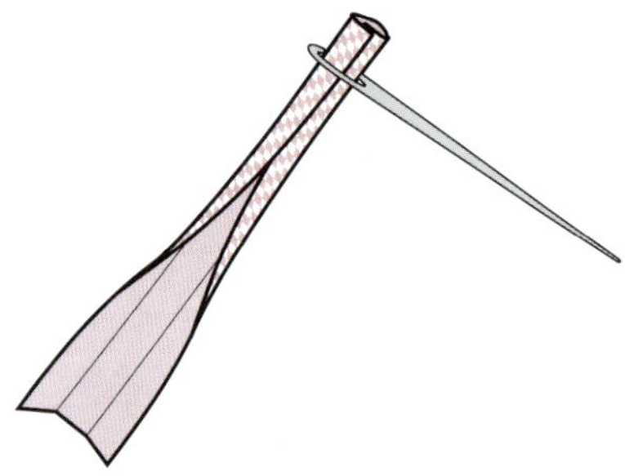

For this technique, the needle should match the width of the ribbon: large embroidery or tapestry needles work perfectly. For example, use a size 26 tapestry needle for ribbons measuring 0.8 to 1.5 inches wide, and a size 24 needle for ribbons of 2.75 inches.

Be sure to pay attention to how you orient the ribbon, to avoid twisting it and to maintain its volume.

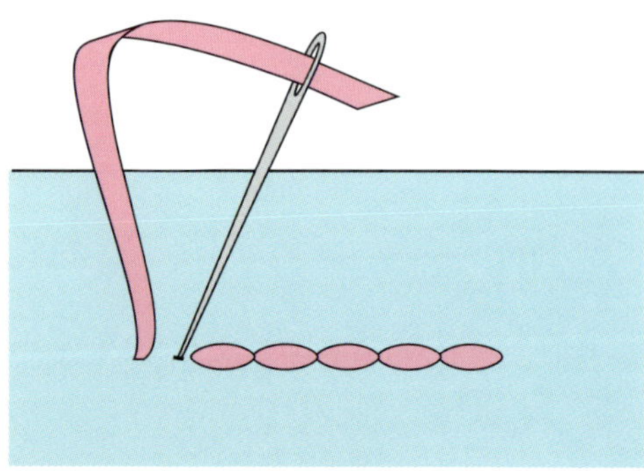

BEADS AND SEQUINS

Embroidering beads or sequins is an easy way to enhance a design. This technique is often used in haute couture.

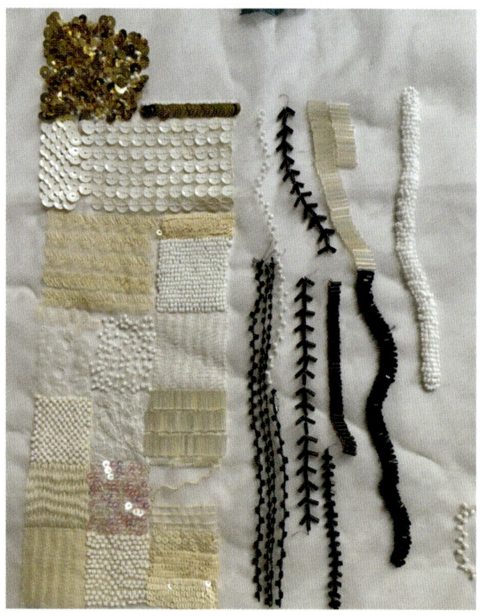

Beaded and sequin pouch (design by Katrin Wiens)

This work is done with a fine needle and thread that matches the color of the bead or sequin

Embroidering beads

1. Insert the needle from the back and bring it out on the front. Pass through the bead and then insert the needle right next to it. Bring the needle out where the next bead will go.

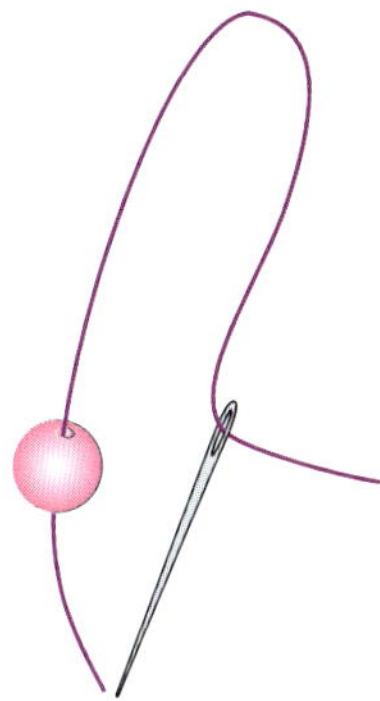

2. If multiple beads are consecutive, sew them in a row, using a backstitch.

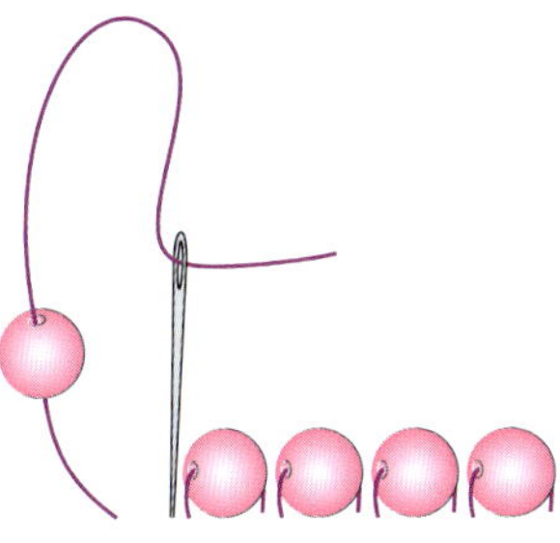

Here's another method for sewing a row of beads: Insert the needle under the fabric, bring it out, thread the beads, and then insert the needle back into the fabric. If the row is long, make a stitch over the thread randomly between the beads or between each bead.

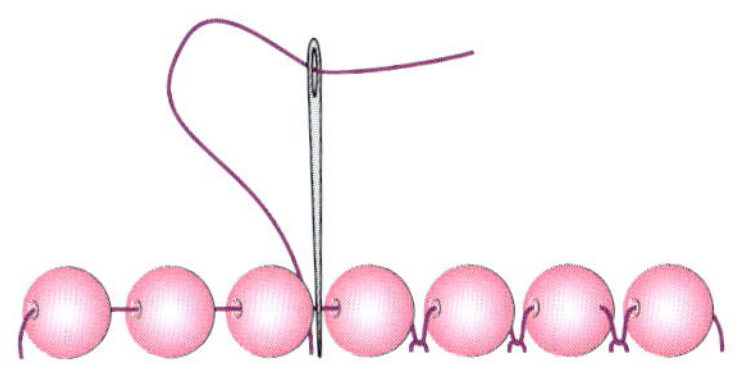

TIP

If you are embroidering a large pearl, to hide the thread with which it is sewn, take out the needle, then pass through the large pearl and then a smaller one.

Pull the thread tight and stitch through the large bead again.

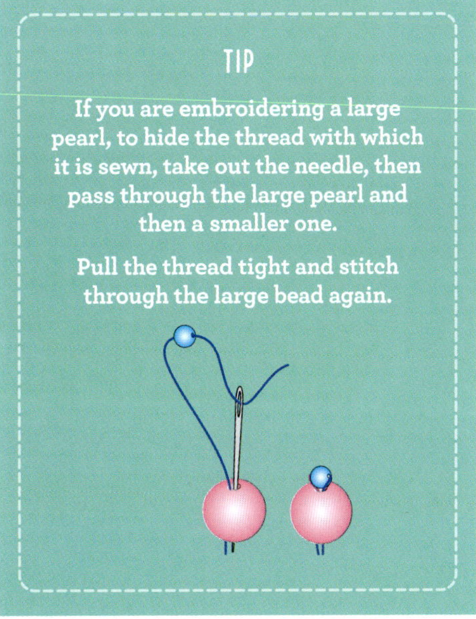

To embroider a loop of beads, start by inserting the needle.

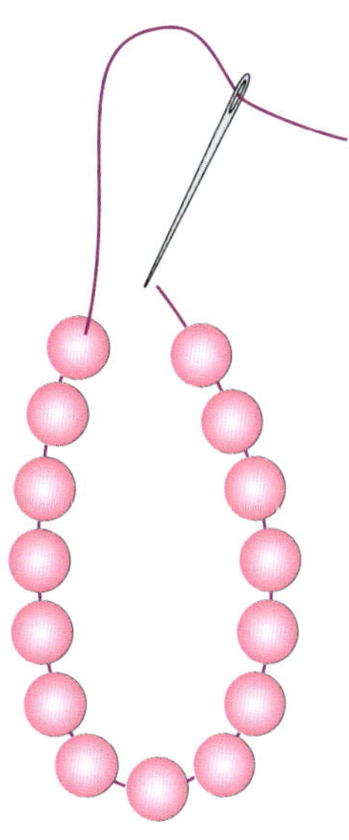

Embroidering Sequins

With backstitch

1. Insert the needle under the fabric, bring it out through the sequin, and stitch to the right.
2. Bring the needle out through the next sequin and stitch between the two sequins.

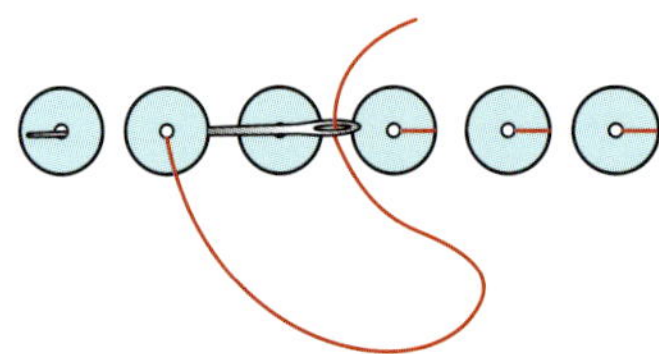

> **TIP**
>
> **To ensure that the sequins lie close together, make a stitch the width of a sequin.**

With two stitches

1. Insert the needle under the fabric, bring it out through the sequin, and stitch to the right.
2. Bring the needle out to the left of this stitch and reinsert it in the same sequin.
3. Bring the needle out through the next sequin to the left.

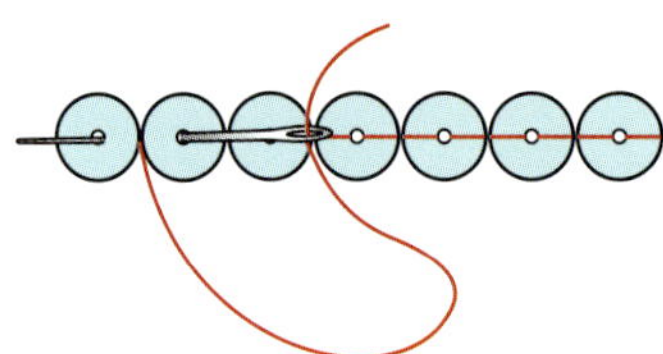

With four stitches

1. Insert the needle under the fabric, bring it out through the sequin, and stitch above it.
2. Bring the needle out through the center and stitch below. Repeat the same on the left and right.

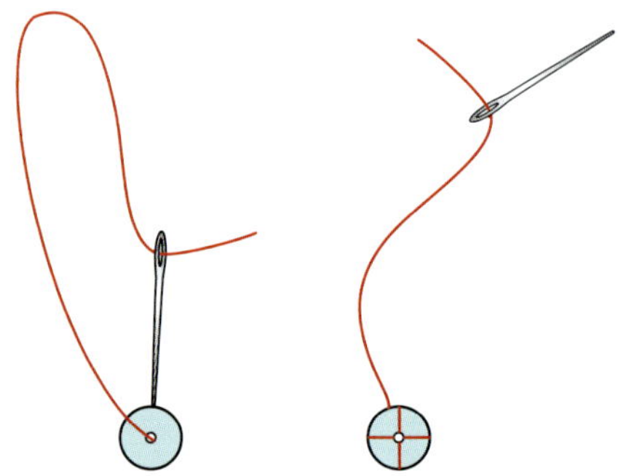

With an invisible stitch

Sew the sequins with a backstitch, folding each sequin to the right as you go to hide the stitches. The sequins should overlap halfway.

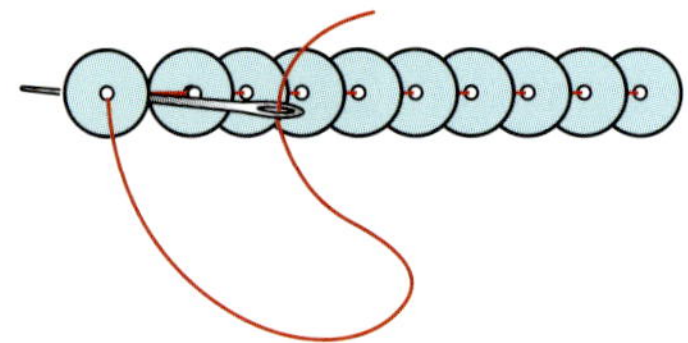

With a bead

1. Insert the needle under the fabric, then bring it out through the sequin and through a bead.
2. Pull the thread tight and stitch back through the sequin.
3. Bring the needle out through the next sequin.

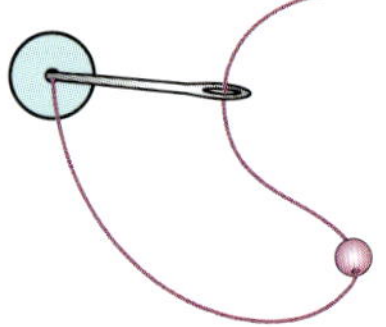

NEEDLEPOINT

Needlepoint is a dense embroidery done on canvas, using wool thread and tapestry needles, which are larger than regular embroidery needles.

This technique is popular with children since the wool and canvas holes are highly visible, making the process quick and accessible.

Contemporary canvas options

Which canvas?

There are two types of canvas:

- **Unifil (monofil) canvas:** This canvas has thick, closely spaced threads and is used mainly for diagonal stitches
- **Penelope (double thread) canvas:** The threads are grouped in pairs horizontally and vertically, making it ideal for straight stitches.

You'll also find preprinted canvases with designs you can fully embroider.

> **WARNING**
>
> **Canvas fabric is very rigid and should not be washed, to avoid distortion.**

Which technique?

A few techniques make working on canvas easier:

1. If the canvas isn't preprinted with a design, draw it on yourself with a fabric marker.
2. Overcast the edges to prevent fraying, leaving a 2-inch margin around the area to be embroidered.
3. Start embroidering from the center to simplify stitch counting.
4. Don't tie knots; instead, leave a 0.8-inch thread tail on the back and cover it with stitches. When finishing, slide the thread under nearby stitches.

Which stitches?

Needlepoint stitches fully cover the canvas and are inspired by classic embroidery stitches. They are stitched in only three directions—horizontal, vertical, or diagonal—but are worked in both directions (one row right to left, then the next row left to right). Mixing directions can help fill shapes more effectively.

> **WARNING**
>
> **Slanted stitches distort the canvas, which then needs to be shaped (see page 60).**

Petit point

This is the most common stitch. It's short and can be embroidered horizontally or vertically.

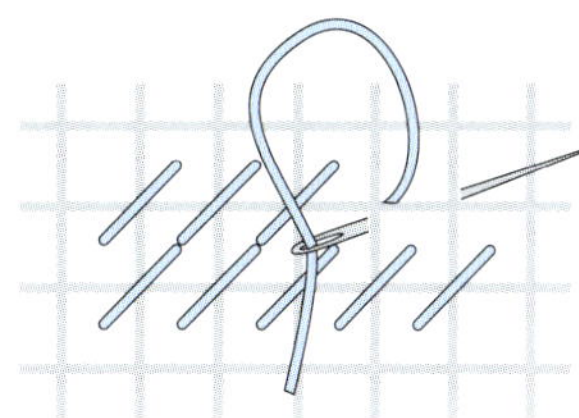

Take care to make your stitches at an angle, since they can distort the canvas.

The cross stitch

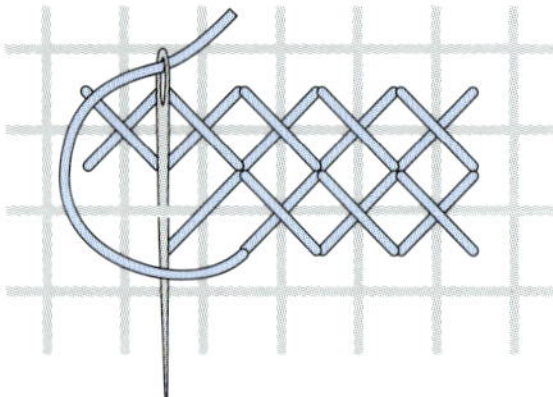

The cross stitch is worked horizontally or vertically (see page 44). Its crossed stitches do not distort the canvas.

Long stitches

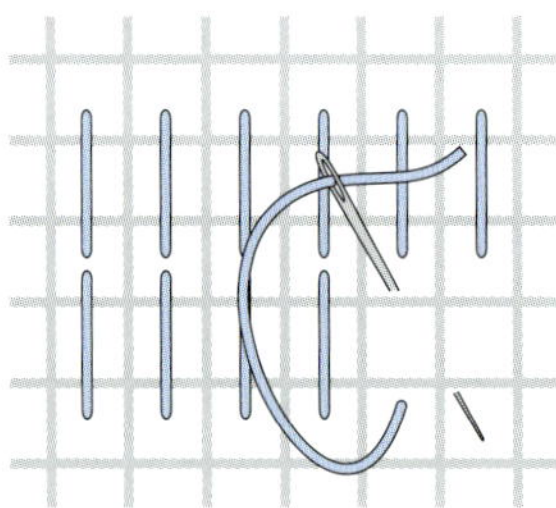

Straight or slanted, long stitches are useful for quickly filling large areas.

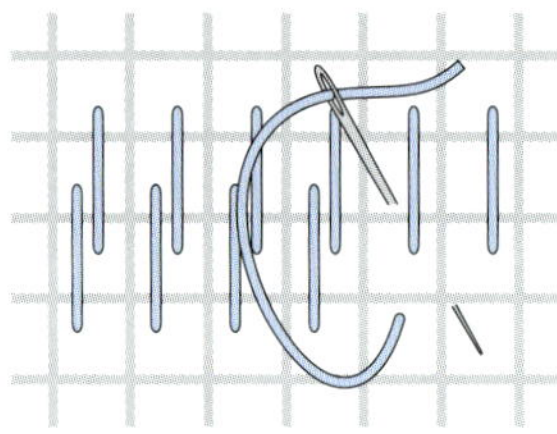

- **Straight gobelin stitch:** Each row is separated from the previous one.
- **Overlapping straight gobelin stitch:** Rows overlap one another.

THE PUNCH NEEDLE

This technique is fun and easy once mastered.

The punch needle is hollow to allow the thread to pass through it and comes in different sizes to match the chosen thread.

Some models are also adjustable in length via a small dial.

The punch needle technique is similar to that used in rug making: The needle is punched into the fabric or canvas, creating loops on the reverse side, while flat stitches appear on the front

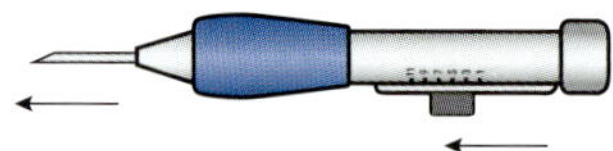

The different stitches

The punch needle requires only one basic stitch, which takes on different forms depending on whether it's viewed from the front or back of the fabric.

- **Flat stitch:** These are stitches made on the front of the fabric and resemble a backstitch.

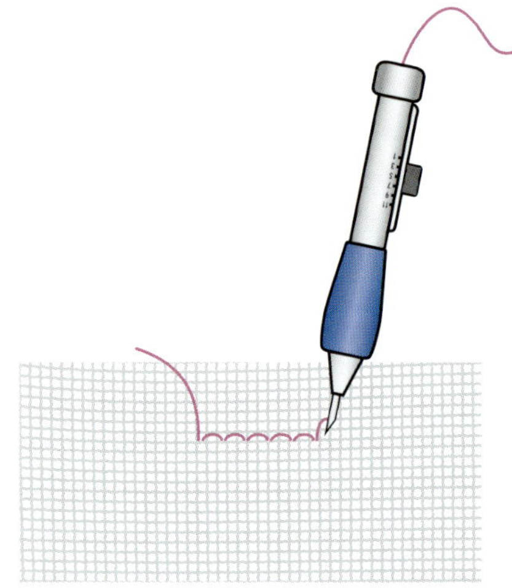

- **Loops:** Loops are small arcs formed on the reverse side, which becomes the visible front. If your needle is adjustable, the loop size varies, measuring half the length of the needle.

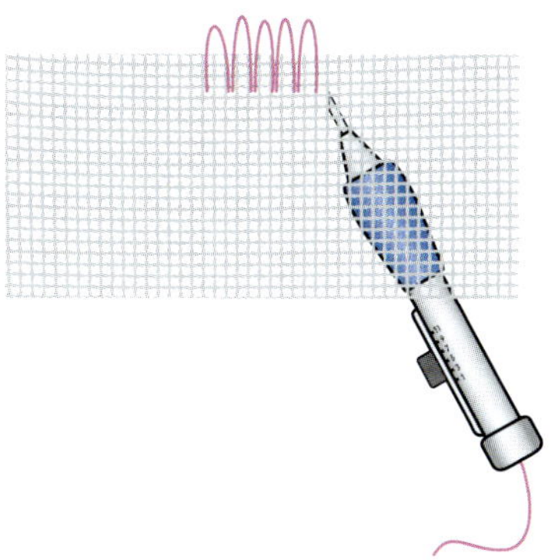

- **Fur effect:** To create a fur effect, simply cut the loops to produce a pile.

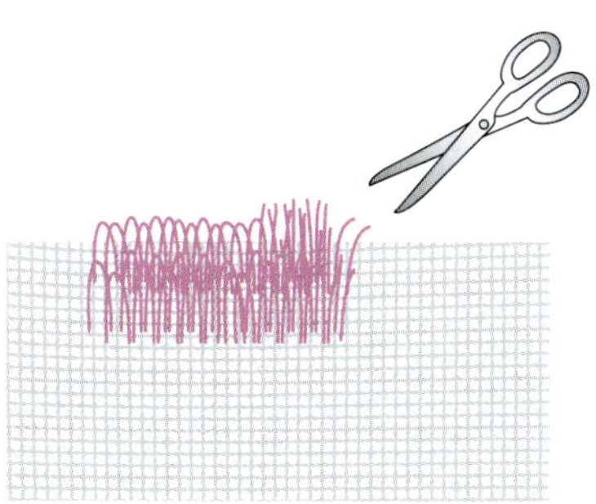

> **TIP**
>
> **If you're working with an adjustable needle, experiment with the stitch length.**

How to embroider

1. Insert the thread through the needle. Refer to the instructions for your specific punch needle model, since threading techniques vary.
2. Insert the fabric into an embroidery hoop.
3. Begin by embroidering the outline of your design. Insert the needle from the front of the fabric while holding 4 inches of thread with your finger. Push the needle fully into the fabric, with the beveled edge pointing toward the next stitch. To adjust the needle direction, turn it while it's in the fabric before pulling it out. This prevents stitches from unraveling.

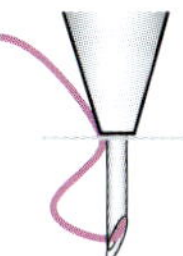

4. Pull the needle out minimally, holding the loop under the fabric with your thumb, without pulling the thread tight, so the loop remains on the opposite side.
5. Insert the needle next to the previous stitch for the next loop. Depending on thread thickness, space stitches no more than 0.5 inches apart.

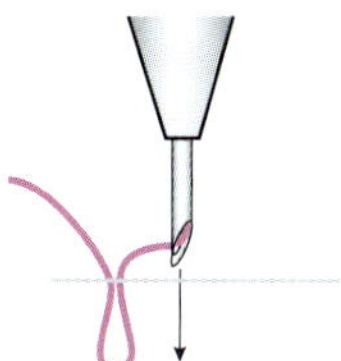

6. Work stitches side by side, following the pattern.

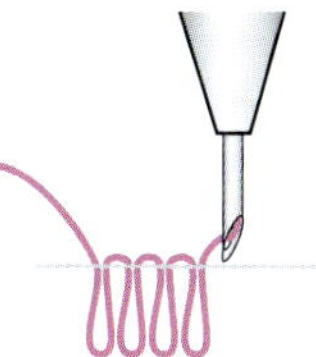

7. Complete the shape, then fill the background. Keep the thread loose at all times to allow loops to form. Unwind the yarn regularly.

8. Once the design is complete or if changing colors, cut the thread, leaving a 4-inch tail. Remove the fabric from the embroidery hoop.

9. Finish by placing an iron-on stabilizing fabric on the reverse side to secure the stitches. Shape it into a geometric form, ensuring it covers all the stitches.

IN CASE OF ERROR

It is very easy to remove a poorly executed stitch by pulling on the thread. But beware—if you pull too much, everything comes undone!

APPLIQUÉ

An appliqué is a piece of fabric (ideally nonfraying) sewn onto another fabric and further embroidered. Here's how to proceed:

1. Trace the design and cut out the fabric, adding a 5 mm margin around the edges. Clip the margins along curves.

2. Pin the appliqué onto the base fabric and sew it with an overcast stitch (see page 24), folding the margins under as you go.

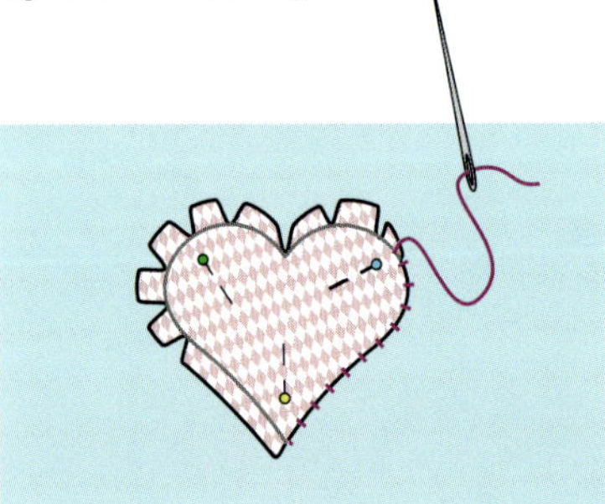

TIP

If you are not comfortable with this technique, turn the margins inside out and baste them before pinning the design to the fabric.

3. Remove the pins. Embroider around the design to conceal the seam, using wide, decorative stitches such as the blanket stitch, buttonhole stitch, feather stitch, chain stitch, or chevron stitch (see page 49).

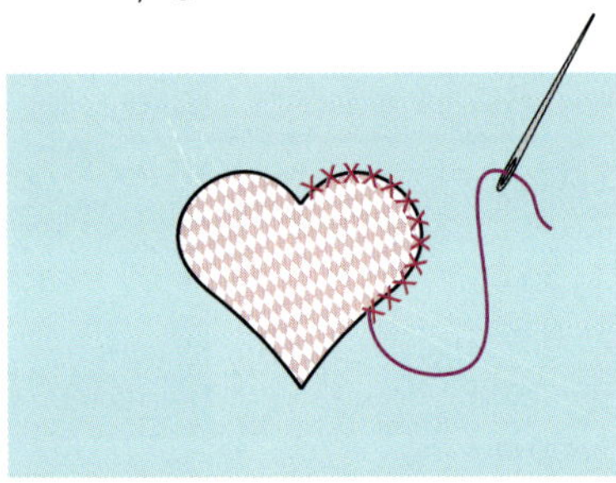

4. Before finishing the seam, you can add a small amount of stuffing inside the appliqué, using a needle for added dimension.

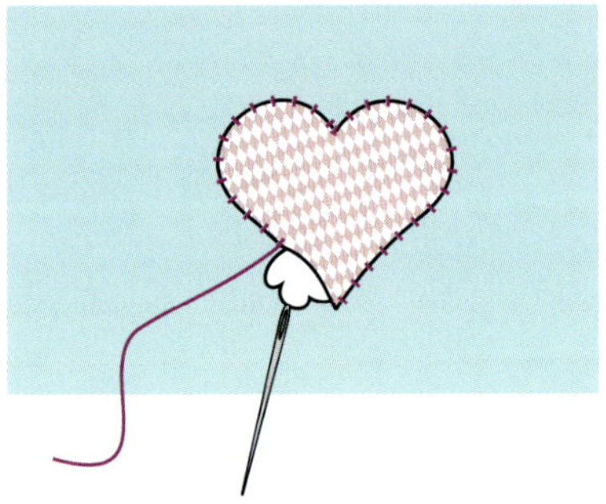

For reverse appliqué, simplyt cut out the design, then cut a slightly larger piece from the appliqué fabric and stitch it behind the opening.

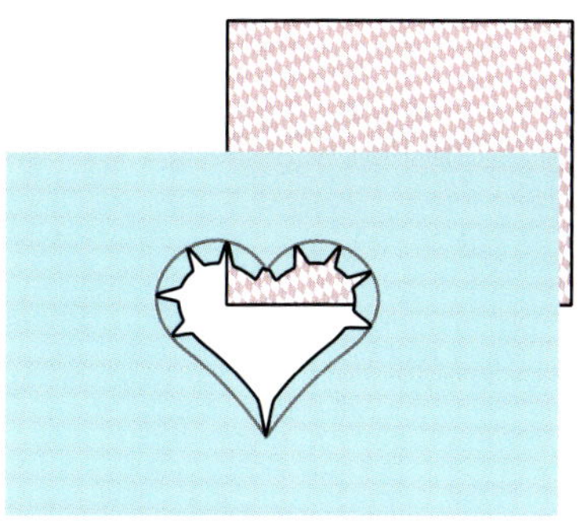

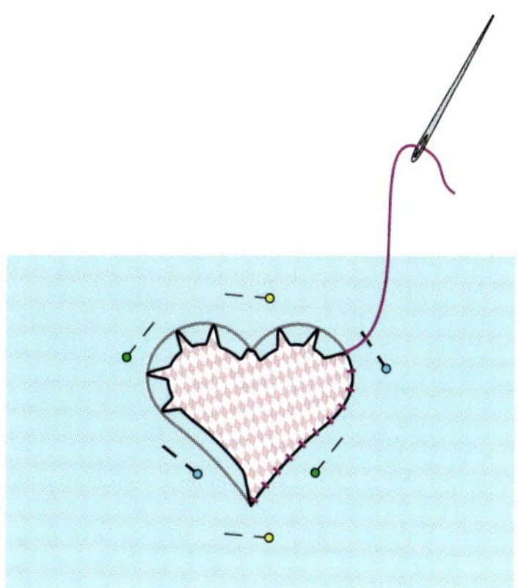

MAKE YOUR OWN PATCHES

1. *Draw a design on a scrap of fabric or felt.*
2. *Outline the design, using a blanket stitch, and fill in the interior with satin stitch or other filling stitches, covering the area fully or partially as desired.*
3. *Using an iron, adhere double-sided fusible webbing to the back of the fabric.*
4. *Cut around the design close to the edge without cutting the stitches.*
5. *Attached the patch by ironing it onto the fabric or sewing it if the fusible webbing isn't double sided.*

If you'd rather not embroider the entire patch, choose a printed fabric and embroider details.

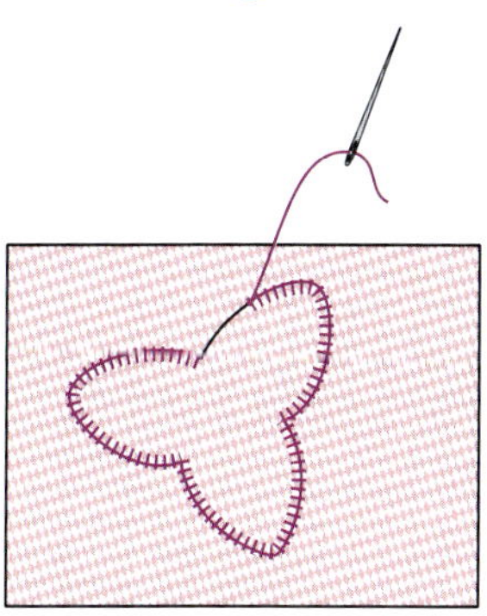

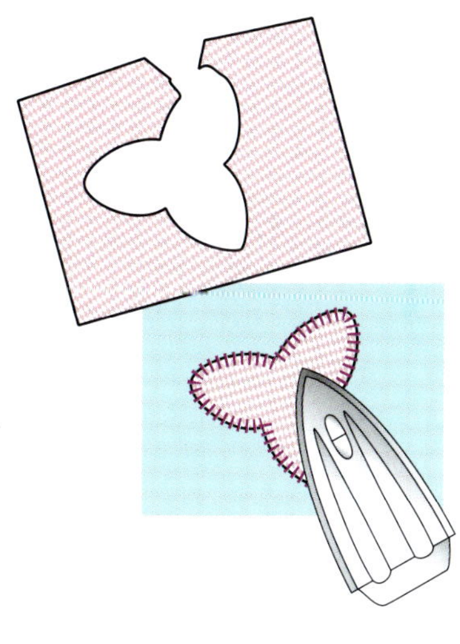

STUMPWORK

In the 17th century, this raised embroidery style was highly popular for decorating boxes and frames.

Flowers in stumpwork

Attached embroidery

With this technique, a raised shape is integrated into the embroidery, allowing you to create elements such as petals or rabbit ears.

1. On the fabric, make three long stitches stretched around a pine.

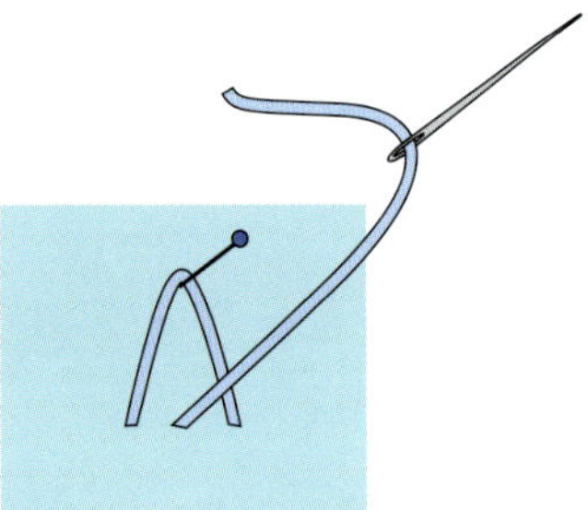

2. Weave over and under the three threads, as if creating a woven structure.

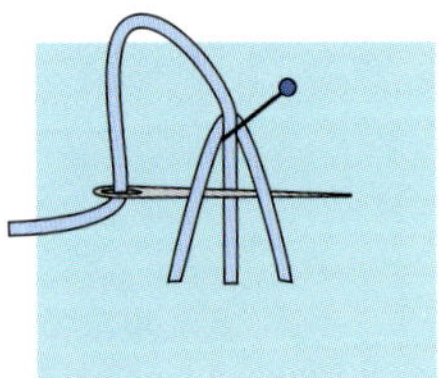

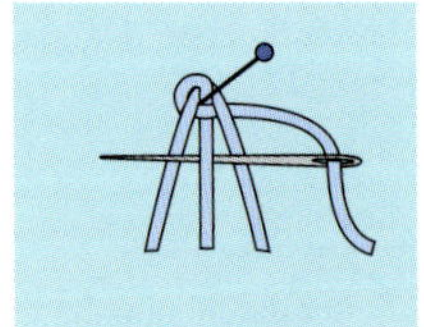

3. Finish by stitching into the fabric and removing the pin.

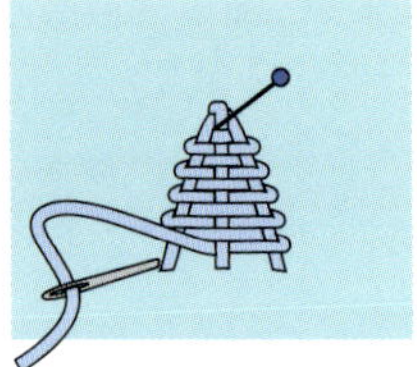

Detached embroidery

This alternative method involves embroidering on a separate piece of fabric, which is then cut out and sewn onto the main embroidery.

1. Draw the shape on the fabric.
2. Thread a very fine wire through the fabric, following the outline of the shape.

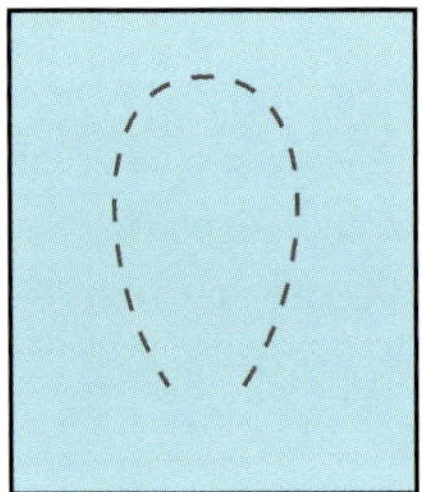

3. Sew over the wire with a tight overcast stitch to create a raised outline.

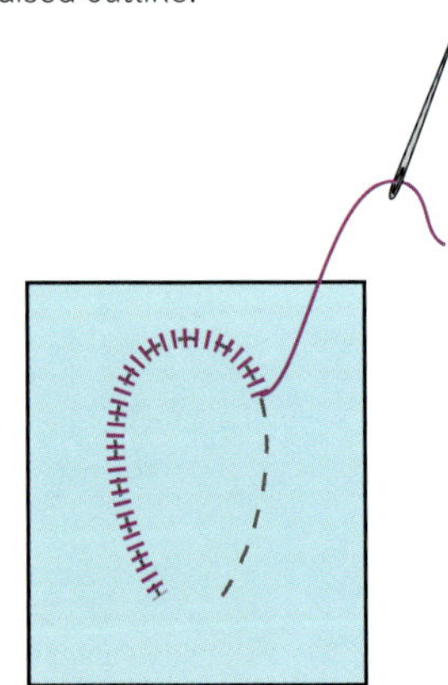

4. Embroider the interior according to the design pattern.

5. Cut the fabric as close as possible to the thread, without cutting the thread.

QUILTING

Quilting involves stitching padding between two layers of fabric, with the stitching often following geometric patterns for decoration. This technique is frequently paired with patchwork to highlight its patterns.

Opaque fabrics are ideal since the reverse side won't show through. Choose soft materials (such as fine cotton) to avoid excessive thickness, and work with a sturdy thread, such as waxed cotton. Be aware that stitching will appear more prominently on a solid-colored fabric.

While often done by machine, quilting can also be hand-stitched using long threads. In this case, a hoop (at least 18 inches in diameter) is helpful to keep the fabric taut.

1. Draw the design on the right side of the backing fabric.
2. Stitch the three layers of fabric together with large stitches.

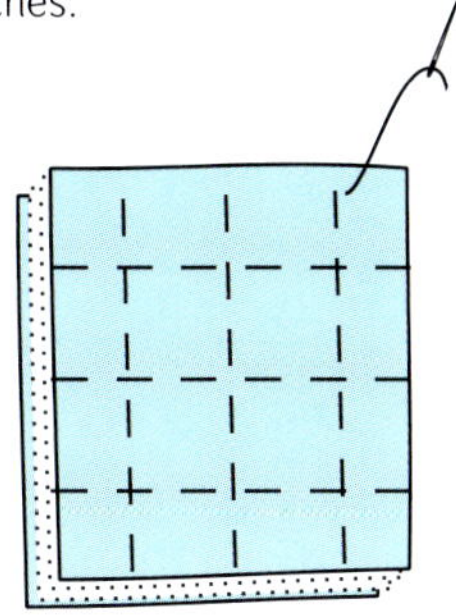

3. Complete the final stitching by hand or machine, following the design's contours. When sewing by hand, use a running stitch with 3 mm stitches.
4. Remove the stitching done in Step 2.

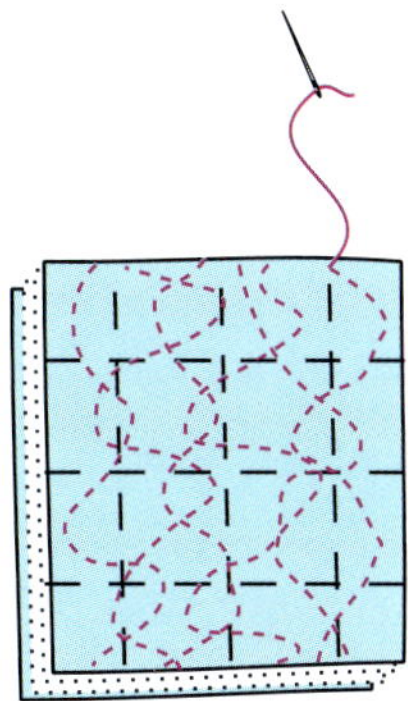

THE BOUTIS TECHNIQUE

The boutis is a variation of quilting and is a style of Provencal stitching that originated in the 17th century, when this type of embroidery arrived from India through the port of Marseille.

The result is elegant, since only the design shapes are filled with cotton wadding, inserted with a large needle. For best results, keep designs small and work with a loosely woven fabric.

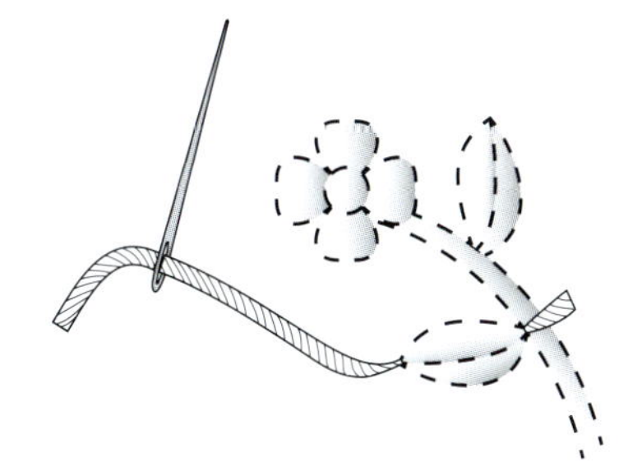

CUTWORK EMBROIDERY

Cutwork embroidery involves stitching closed motifs and then cutting out sections with scissors. Originally, English embroidery was made in this style.

Embroidered collar with beads and cutwork (design by Les Beaux Arts du Fil)

1. Choose a tightly woven fabric that won't fray, and trace the design onto it.
2. Outline the design with a running stitch, then embroider over it with a blanket stitch.

TIP

To avoid mistakes, draw an X in each area to be hollowed out.

3. Carefully cut out the inner fabric sections, using small, sharp scissors.

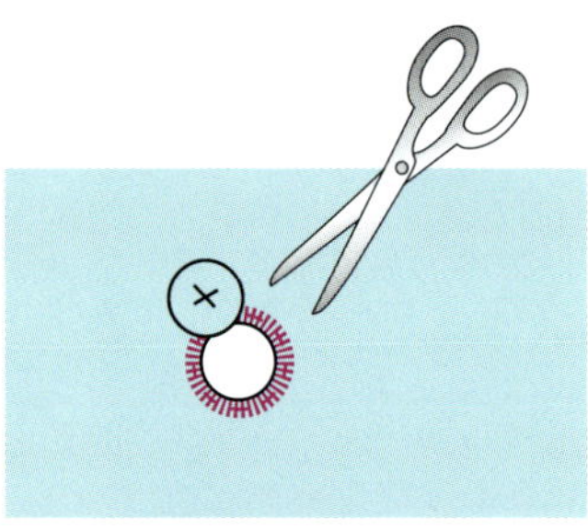

SCALLOPED STRAPS

To join openwork sections, make scalloped straps before adding the pattern.

1. Mark the contours of the first part of the design to be open-worked in front stitch, and embroider three cast-on stitches between the two lines, over the fabric.

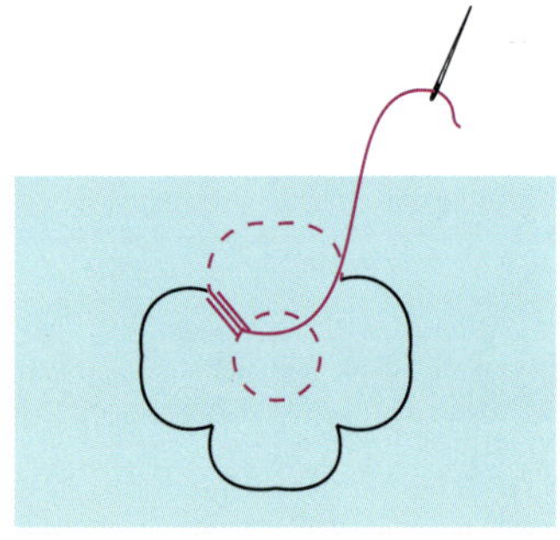

2. Make a scalloped stitch on these three castoff stitches, without using the fabric.

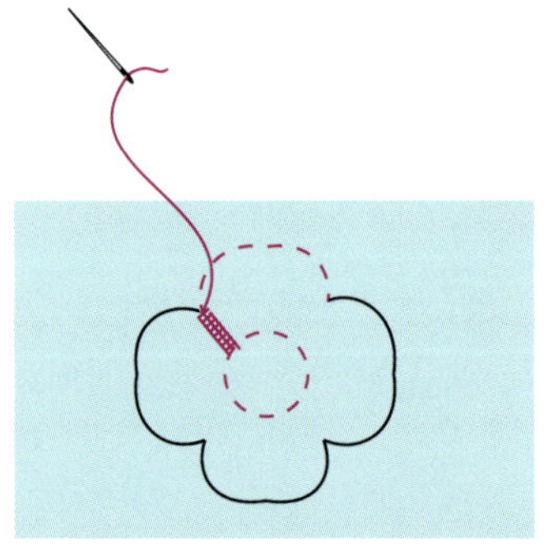

3. Continue to mark the design in front stitch until you reach the next bridle. Cover with blanket stitches. Cut the fabric from behind, without touching the straps.

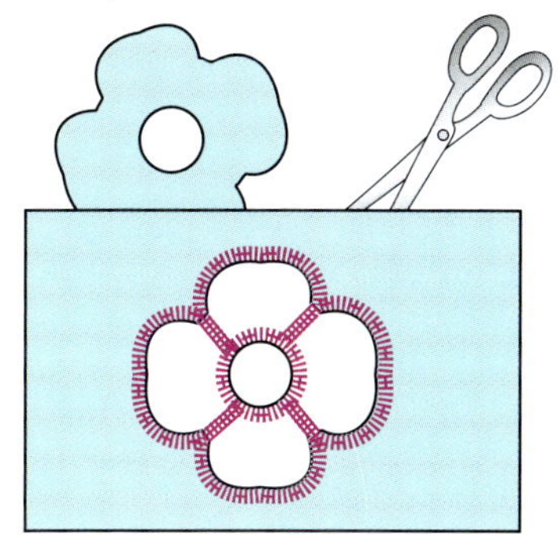

DRAWN-THREAD EMBROIDERY

This technique is often used to conceal hem seams. The cutwork stitching is completed by removing horizontal threads to create open bands, while grouping vertical threads to form patterns.

It is best done on fabrics with thick, evenly woven threads, such as linen. Use embroidery thread of the same thickness and a needle suited to the thread size.

Tablecloth with drawn-thread hem

How to draw threads

1. Outline the band to be cutwork-embroidered with a basting stitch. Determine the number of threads to be removed based on the stitch type. For example, if the stitch groups three threads, the total thread count should be divisible by three. This guideline applies to all stitches.

NOTE

Threads are grouped together to form a bundle, generally composed of three to five threads.

2. Cut the horizontal threads in the center of the band, close to the basting stitch. Using a needle or tweezers, pull them to the band's ends and tuck them into the fabric with a needle.

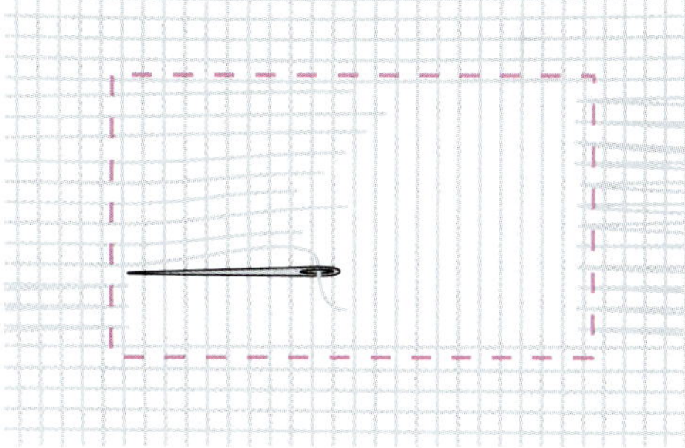

How to stitch the drawn threads

Here are some simple stitches for edging the bands and gathering the thread bundles. You can adapt them to many variations. To start and end your embroidery, make an overcast stitch (see page 24) on the fabric.

Simple drawn-thread stitches

Simple drawn-thread stitches are stitched from left to right along only one edge of the band.

1. Insert the needle under the fabric and make a small overcast stitch along the edge. Bring it out to the left of the threads.

2. Pass the needle from right to left behind the threads to bundle them, then stitch to the right from the back.

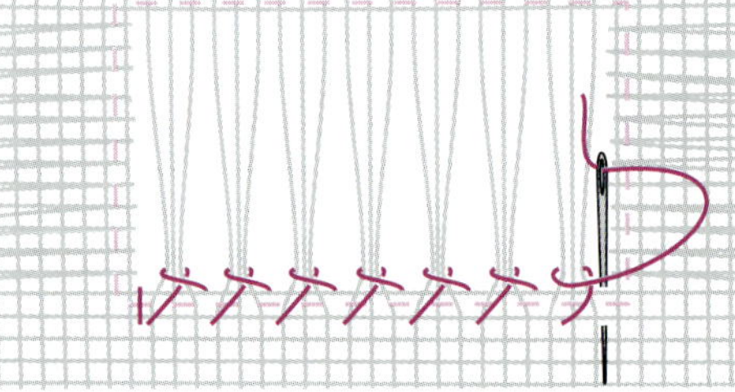

3. Repeat for the next bundle.

Ladder hemstitching

These are single drawn-thread stitches done on both the top and bottom of the band.

1. Complete the single drawn-thread stitches along the top edge.
2. Turn the fabric around and repeat the process along the bottom, using the same bundles.

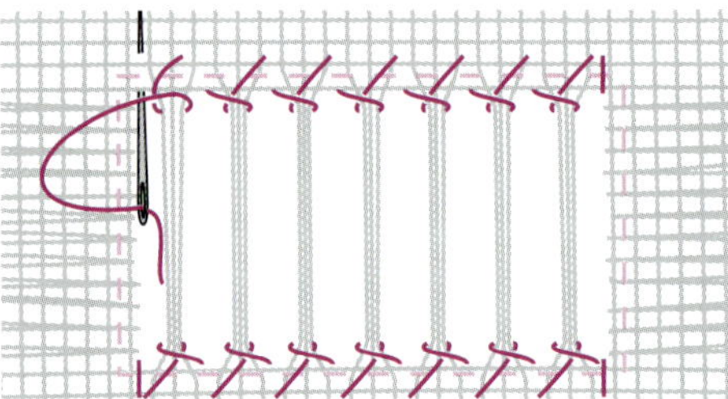

River hemstitching

This style requires an even number of threads in each bundle.

1. Stitch the top edge as in single drawn-thread stitches.

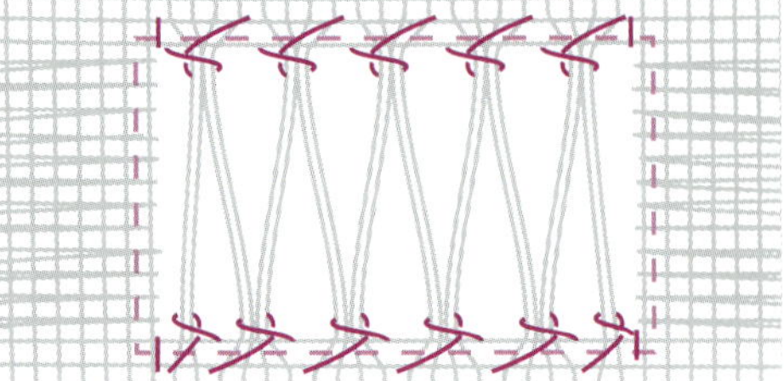

2. Flip the work and stitch the bottom edge, taking half the threads from one bundle and half from the next.

Venetian hemstitching

To move from one bundle to the next, stitch from top to bottom and back up.

1. Wrap the thread tightly around each bundle.
2. Stitch into the edge.

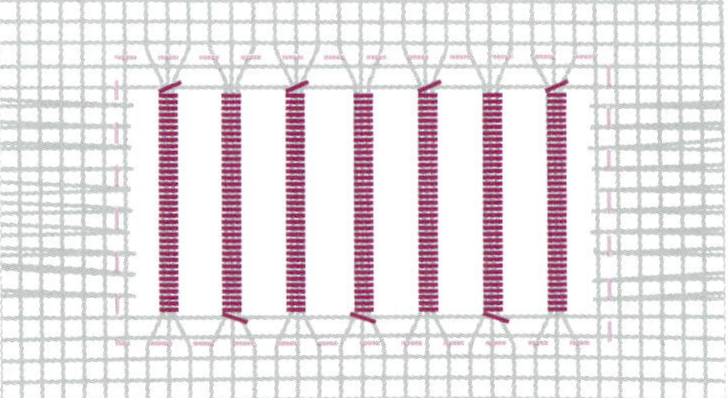

Quick hemstitching

This hemstitch style is stitched from right to left.

1. Insert the needle under the fabric at the center of the openwork section and make an overcast stitch.
2. Pass the needle from back to front, wrapping around the threads of the first bundle.
3. Before tightening, pass the needle through the loop to create a knot.

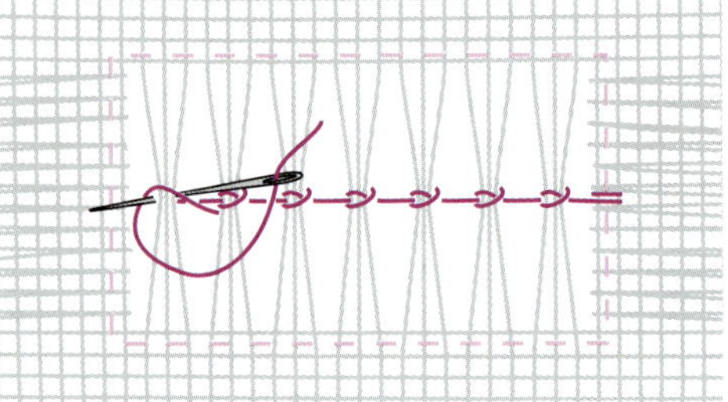

Knotted bundles

This stitch follows the same process as the quick hemstitch but groups bundles together.

1. Work a ladder hemstitch by wrapping multiple threads to create bundles.
2. Repeat, this time wrapping multiple bundles instead of single threads.

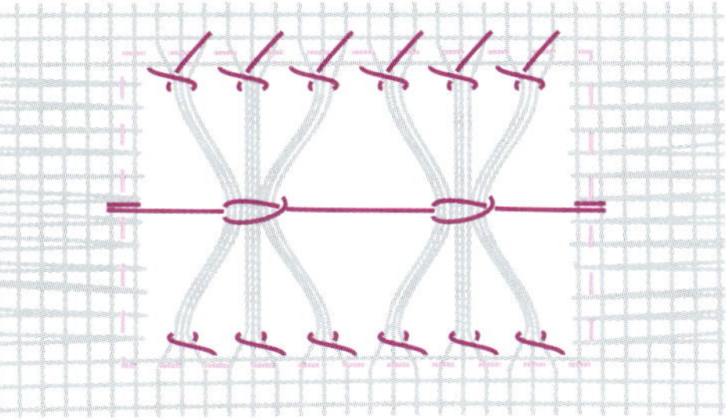

Crossed bundles

Crossed bundles are stitched from right to left. Simply cross pairs of bundles by passing the needle over the second bundle and under the first, keeping the thread taut.

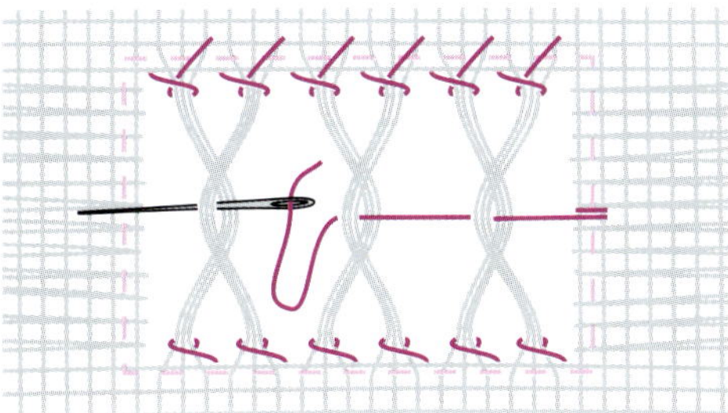

SMOCKING

This decorative embroidery dates back to the Middle Ages and was originally used to create loose work blouses. Today, it's seen mostly on children's clothing and summer dresses.

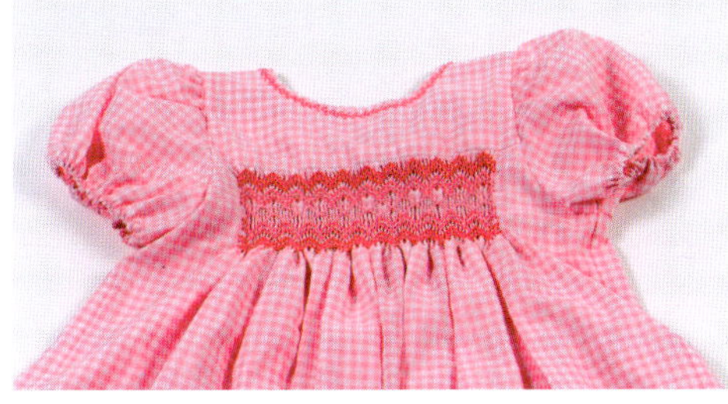

Child's dress with smocking

Light cotton is ideal for smocking, using one, two, or three strands of embroidery thread (depending on the fabric) with an embroidery needle.

Creating the gathers

The fabric needs to be gathered before embroidering. Start with fabric three times the width of the finished piece and allow at least 1 inch of extra space around the gathered area.

1. On the reverse side, mark a dotted grid with spaces between 1.2 to 2.5 inches, depending on fabric thickness.

TIP

Using a fabric printed with small patterns means you don't have to trace the dotted grid. Just follow the patterns.

2. Stitch a small running stitch along each dot, leaving a 4-inch thread tail at the end of each row.

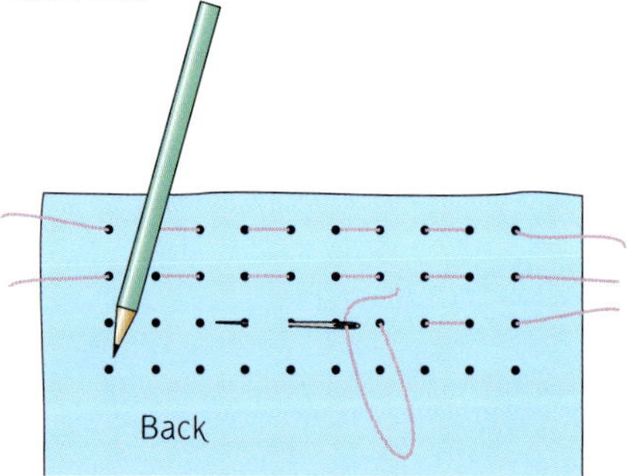

3. Pull the threads on both sides to gather the fabric until it's slightly narrower than the desired final width. Knot each pair of threads. The fabric will expand slightly when the gathering threads are removed.

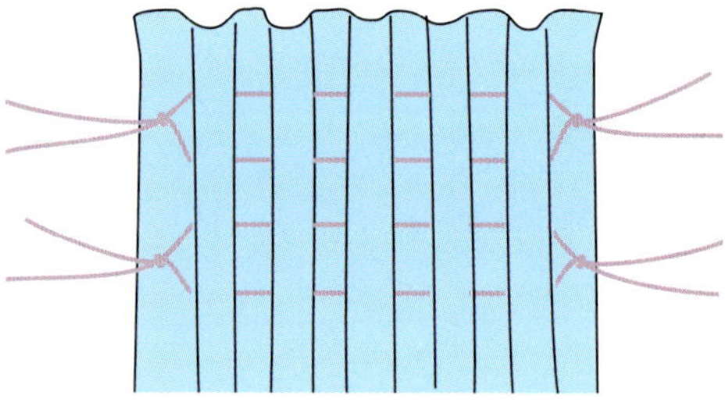

4. Spread out the gathers evenly by hand.

Embroidering

Work along the gathered lines from left to right, making one stitch per fold.

> **NOTE**
>
> **The stitches must be embroidered just above or below the gathering lines, so that they can easily be removed later.**

Various stitches are suitable:

- **The stem stitch** (see page 39): This simple stitch involves making one stitch in each fold.

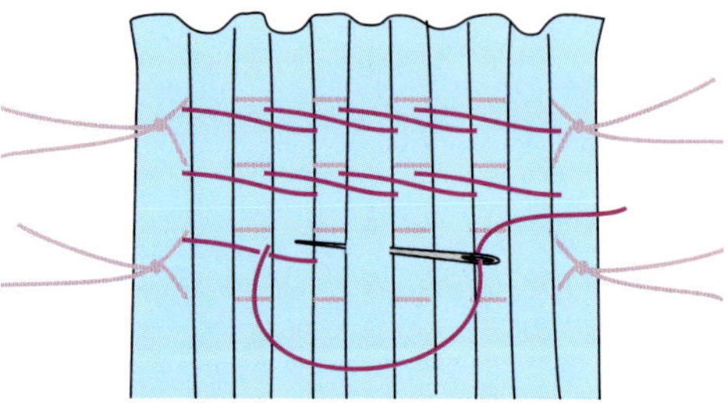

- **The cable stitch:** Worked from left to right, make a backstitch (see page 38), taking in two folds. Place the next stitch directly below, shifting by one fold. Alternate stitches above and below to create a cable effect.

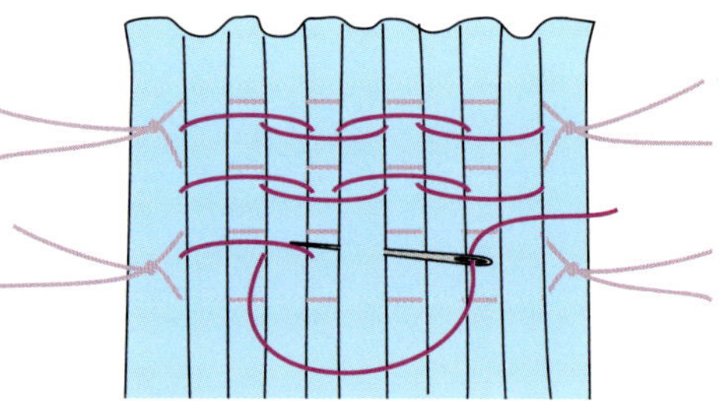

- **The honeycomb stitch:** A variation of the cable stitch; use a double backstitch to take in two folds, then a double stitch on the next gathered line below, shifting by one fold each time.

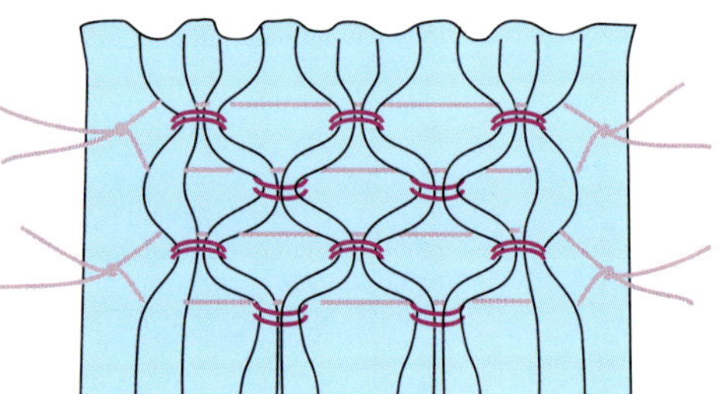

- **The blanket stitch** (see page 52): Work from left to right, taking two folds with each stitch.

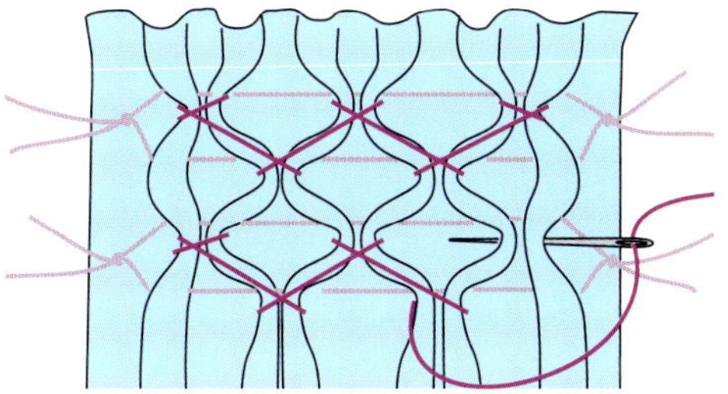

MACHINE EMBROIDERY

Both dedicated embroidery machines and standard home sewing machines can be used to cover large areas, such as tablecloths, or for quilting.

The embroidery machine

Ideal for precise patterns, borders, repetitive designs, or text, embroidery machines can also quilt (see page 77).

They operate like domestic sewing machines but come with built-in embroidery designs, programmable through a screen, allowing the machine to stitch the pattern automatically.

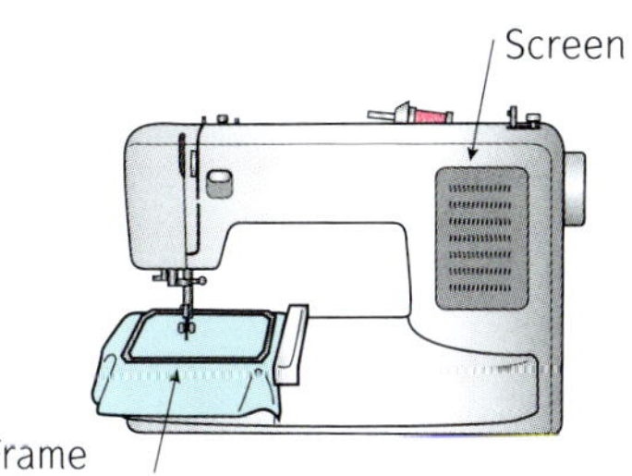

> **DID YOU KNOW?**
>
> **The price of the embroidery machine depends on the size of the surface to be embroidered, the screen, and the number of designs.**

The domestic sewing machine

With basic stitches, you can also embroider with a home sewing machine.

For geometric designs, stitch normally. For free-form designs, use the free-motion technique, guiding the fabric manually to draw as you sew.

Lower the feed dogs (the teeth that move the fabric beneath the presser foot) or cover them with a plate as per your machine's instructions.

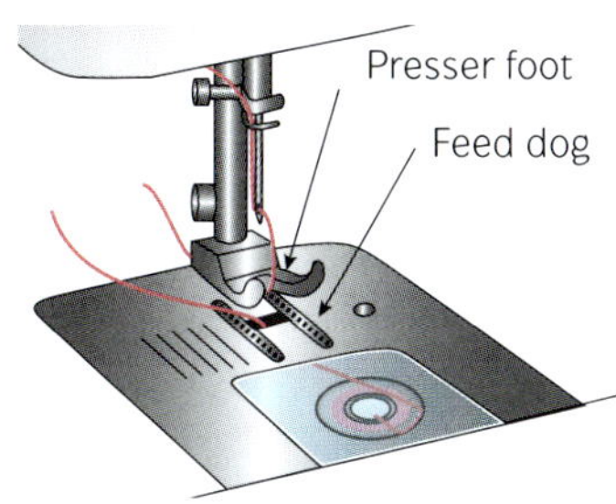

Special presser feet for free-motion stitching are available and compatible with most machine brands.

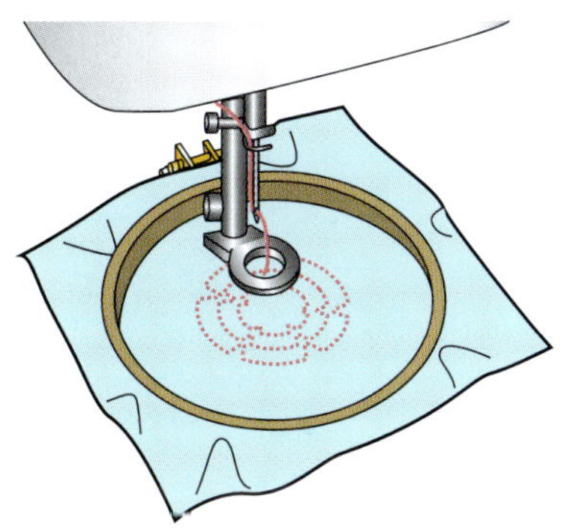

APPENDIXES

STITCH-COUNT CONVERSION TABLE

In France, stitches are calculated as the number of stitches or threads per centimeter:

- On linen or cheesecloth, you count in threads/cm (number of threads per centimeter);
- On some fabrics (such as Aïda), stitches are counted in pts./cm (number of stitches per centimeter).

In English-speaking countries, counts are used (stitches per inch). This table will help you convert these measurements.

Aïda cloth	
11 counts	4.4 pts. / cm
14 counts	5.5 pts. / cm
16 counts	6.3 pts. / cm
18 counts	7.2 pts. / cm
Linen fabric	
28 counts	11 threads / cm
32 counts	12 threads / cm
35 counts	14 threads / cm
40 counts	16 threads / cm

SOLUTIONS TO COMMON PROBLEMS

My thread gets twisted

At some point, the strands of the thread may start to tangle or separate during your work. If that happens, turn the hoop over and let the needle hang at the end of the thread. It will naturally spin until the strands are back in order.

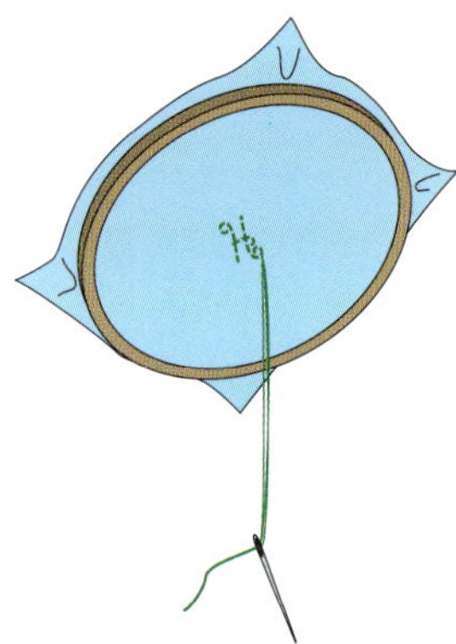

I don't have enough thread

Running a bit low on thread and can't wait to buy more? You don't have to stitch every point or fill in all the surfaces; the result will still look beautiful!

You can also make up for the missing thread by mixing strands from two other colors: for example, to get six strands of purple, twist together three strands of pink and three strands of blue.

If you're only short of thread required for tying the knot at the end of the embroidery, separate the strands and knot them together. Make sure the knot doesn't slip through the fabric.

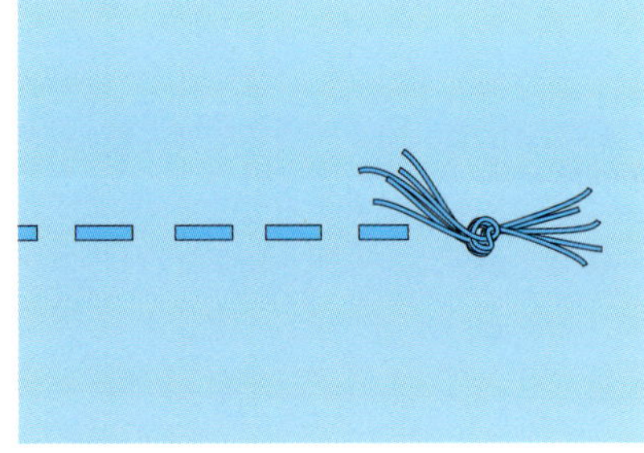

My fabric is too thin or too soft

Iron a piece of fusible fabric or stabilizer onto the back (see page 20).

I have dry hands

Dry hands can cause the thread to snag and wear down. Use a bit of hand cream to keep them moisturized.

PARTNERSHIPS AND ACKNOWLEDGMENTS

DMC

www.dmc.com

I would like to thank DMC for all the embroidery threads, needles, hoops, canvas, and accessories.

Ma Petite Mercerie

www.mapetitemercerie.com

I would also like to thank Ma Petite Mercerie for the fabrics other than the embroidery canvas.

Les Beaux Arts du Fil

http://lesbeauxartsdufil.com

For photos of embroidery work and information about the Lunéville Borderie, thanks to Claire Liotta, director of the Ecole internationale de broderie d'art.

Les Beaux Arts du Fil

Katrin Wiens

katrinwiens.com

For photos of embroidery work, thanks to Katrin Wiens, fashion designer.

INDEX

A

appliqué work, 74–75

B

backstitch, 20, 38, 39, 69, 70, 72, 82

blanket stitch, 49, 74, 75, 78, 79, 83

brick stitch, 57

buttonhole stitch, 49, 74

C

canvas, 8–12, 19, 24, 26, 28, 60, 71

chain stitch, 39, 74

chalk, 8, 14

color reference, 12, 22, 31

contemporary embroidery, 71

cotton, 8, 10, 11, 27, 60, 63, 77, 81

cotton thread, 8, 13, 31

couching, 41

counted threads, 8, 9, 11, 22, 25, 87

cross stitch, 9, 10, 19, 20, 22, 33, 44–45, 48, 53, 54, 55, 72

cutwork embroidery, 78–79

D

darning stitch, 53

double cross stitch, 45

double rice stitch, 43

drawn-thread embroidery, 79–81

E

embroidery needles, 8, 13, 71, 81

F

feather stitch, 50–51, 74

fern stitch, 47

French knot, 48

H

half cross stitch, 54–55

hemstitching, 80

I

interfacing fabric, 24, 65

K

knotted stitch, 34–35

L

lattice stitch, 57

lazy daisy stitch, 48

linen, 9, 11, 60, 79, 87

long-armed cross stitch, 53

looped stem stitch, 40

M

machine embroidery, 13, 60, 61, 77, 83

Magic canvas, 10

Magic needle, 14

mono needlepoint, 71

monogramming, 20

N

needlepoint, 71–72

O

open backstitch, 38

overcast stitch, 24, 64, 71, 74, 76, 79, 80

P

pearl needle, 14

perle cotton, 8, 13, 31

Persian stitch, 52

petit point, 22, 71

plaited stitch, 52

Provençal quilting, 77

punch needle, 14, 72–74

Q

quilting, 28, 77, 83

R

raised work, 33, 40, 65, 76

reversible cross stitch, 55

ribbon embroidery, 68

running stitch, 22, 38, 40, 64, 77, 78, 82

S

satin stitch, 56–57, 75

sheaf stitch, 42

silk, 13

single fly stitch, 47

slip stitch, 40

smocking, 81–83

star stitch, 45–46

stem stitch, 20, 39–40, 82

straight stitch, 41–42, 45, 57, 61, 71

stumpwork, 76–77

T

tapestry needles, 13

W

water-soluble transfer pen, 8, 14

web stitch, 46

whipped running stitch, 40

wool, 13, 71

woven hemstitching, 80

Embroidery thread is made up of several strands.

Depending on the size of the thread used (i.e., the number of strands chosen), the final appearance of the embroidery will vary. The smaller the design, the finer the thread.

But don't embroider with just any thread! Go for embroidery threads that won't wear out or fade.